THE OTHER SIDE OF JORDAN

THE
OTHER SIDE
OF
JORDAN

By Harry S. Ashmore

W·W·NORTON & COMPANY · INC · New York

For Barbara

CONTENTS

INTRODUCTION

I T HAS always seemed to me that the bare biographical
data pertinent to one who was born and raised in the
South, practiced journalism there for more than two
decades, and lived through Little Rock, should provide a
satisfactory answer to the recurring question: How did
you happen to become interested in race relations?

The subject is not one I took up as a hobby, or in which
I have a separate, sentimental interest. It is, rather, a matter I have not been able to avoid. The mere existence of
the Negro minority in my native region—unassimilated
and never justly accommodated—was and is a dominant
fact of Southern life. The region's peculiar institutions
were erected around it, the distinctive Southern attitude
determined by it. No one can really ignore the problems
attendant to this condition, although most of us have
tried, and thereby have compounded them.

There is, of course, a rational solution—simply to treat

9

the Negro as we treat everyone else and permit him to find his own level in a society presumably based on equalitarian concepts of freedom and justice. But, unhappily, this is an emotional, not a rational matter. White people come to it equipped with a full set of formless fears and out of these, almost everywhere in the world, they have fashioned racist philosophies and restrictive social devices. These, naturally, are hard on the Negro, but they are also hard on the white man. They force him to an unremitting and generally unsatisfactory examination of his conscience, unless he shields it with an insensitivity that keeps out the shining pleasures of the spirit along with the pangs of guilt. The peculiar institutions have had practical consequences, too; in defense of slavery and its successor, forced segregation, the South lost a war and withdrew from the main stream of history. While America grew rich and strong the American South remained poor, scorned, and beset by demagogues.

It does not, as I have suggested, make a great deal of sense that this has been so. There is splendid irony in the fact that the submerged and exploited tenth of the American people should have shaped so much of the nation's history—not by positive action on their own motion, but simply by being present, and this initially against their will. Had there been no Negro there would have been no South; had there been no South there would have been no Civil War; had there been no Civil War and Reconstruction there would have been no regional one-party system with its profound, continuing influence on national politics and public policy. No one can be sure whether our unfolding history would have been happier under these circumstances, but certainly it would have been different.

The thought is of some moment in this season when Civil War buffs are proliferating at their round tables and marching by proxy across the dark and bloody ground of a century ago. It is possible that the current national obsession with the campaigns of Lee and Grant and their lieutenants is a kind of romantic retreat from the harsh reality of the mid-century. A man who can attune the inner ear to the echo of bugles signaling a cavalry charge at Antietam may be able to ignore the count-down at Cape Canaveral. And by concentrating on the glory of dead generals and the agony of forgotten privates he is able to detach this segment of history from the snarl of conflicting social, political, and economic forces that produced the great fratricide—and from the historical continuum that runs from the arrival of the first slave ship through Appomattox to last year's, this year's and next year's footless Congressional debate on civil rights.

I do not begrudge the anesthetic pleasure of those who are able to indulge in protracted speculation over how it might have been had Van Dorn had one more regiment at

Pea Ridge. I only note that in my case it has been denied me by circumstance. As the centenary of my grandfathers' war approached it turned out that I had to contend with the here and now, in the formidable person of Orval Faubus. If the exercise was exhausting it was also instructive. It was possible to demonstrate, by a process of simple logic, that most of the horses Faubus chose to flay with his oratorical whips were long since dead, and some in fact had never drawn the breath of life. But it was also possible for Faubus to demonstrate in practice that palpable absurdity does not invalidate a deeply-held human fear—in this case the fear that somehow the flowering civilization of Arkansas had been subverted by a hostile central government and was about to be engulfed by a rising tide of blacks hell-bent on miscegenation. The emotions thus engendered are far too complex to be written down as simple race prejudice. This alone would not, I think, prompt a people to invite disaster, suffer it, and conclude that they had won a famous victory.

If such aberrations were confined to Southern whites, as most Americans comfortably believed through much of our history, they would hardly deserve more than passing curiosity. It is already quite clear that Orval Faubus has no importance except as a symbol, and leads no movement of real significance to the chronicle of our time. Indeed, in sum total, the clamorous dislocations across the South in the wake of the Supreme Court's school deci-

sions are of little practical import in a world civilization that is literally reaching toward the stars and has
already touched the moon. In any event, the South is pay-
ing in the coin of steadily diminishing national political
influence for the mingled pleasure and pain of what is
likely to be its last stand.

But the not yet fully recognized fact is that the race
problem is no longer the exclusive or even the primary
property of the South, and neither is the resistant white
attitude normally associated with the beleaguered region.
The 1960 census will show that more than half of America's Negroes now live outside the Confederate states.
The great migration began around the time of World
War I, was slowed by the depression years, and resumed
with new force during World War II and its affluent
aftermath. This mass movement doubtless has been stim-
ulated to some degree by the social and political protest
of the period, but its base is primarily economic. In the
great industrial centers the expanding economy has created a vacuum at the bottom of the labor pool; it has been
filled from the only sources available since barriers were
erected against European and Asian immigration—by
underemployed Negroes from the South, and by Spanish-
speaking Puerto Ricans from the nation's Caribbean commonwealth.

For the Negro the transition involves a great deal more
than geography. Usually at one stroke, he has moved from

the land, which gave him his sustenance and much of his culture, to the heart of a great city. Here he has found the paternalism of the South, which was a source of protection as well as of resentment, replaced by indifference. And at the point of social contact with whites he has often re-encountered the overt hostility he hoped to leave behind when he crossed over Jordan in search of the Promised Land.

This book, then, is about Negroes who have settled outside the South—those who have a generation or more of urban living behind them, the newcomers who continue to stream in to swell the population of the Northern ghettos, and, only incidentally, about the Puerto Ricans with whom they share the city slums under a sort of uneasy truce.

The work is not the product of my original inspiration. It was prompted by an old friend and colleague who is himself a recent migrant—Robert M. White II, summoned lately from his labors on his family newspaper at Mexico, Missouri, to serve as president and editor of the *New York Herald Tribune*. Reflecting upon the complex nature of his new circulation territory, White concluded that someone should take a dispassionate look at the colored 20 per cent of the population which causes a good deal of anxiety among the rest even while, for practical purposes, remaining largely invisible. In a remarkable demonstration of his persuasive powers, he convinced me that I should assume the task. My own rationalization for taking up again a burden I thought I had finally put down was recognition that, after all, this was an essential and largely unexamined part of the running story that had occupied much of my attention throughout my journalistic career. After Harlem, as another editor remarked in tendering me a proposition I have so far managed to resist, there would be nothing left but Johannesburg.

What follows is an expanded version of twelve articles published in April, 1960, in the *Herald Tribune* and distributed through its syndicate to 25 major American newspapers, including, it should be noted, several in the South. It is, unabashedly, journalism. I make no claim to scientific method. I simply went and looked and listened in the places Negroes of all conditions live in our biggest city, and talked before and after these visitations with some of those, white and colored, in New York and elsewhere, who have had long experience with the urban problem. I brought to the assignment whatever capacity for observation and interpretation I have acquired out of varied experience as reporter and editor and, I hope, qualities of compassion and understanding that reflect my genuine regard for a people who have always astounded me with their capacity for amiability and tolerance under duress.

It is a measure of the great void between the white and

Negro communities that such an investigation would have been inordinately time-consuming, and perhaps impossible, for a white man traveling alone. There are public and private agencies that provide abundant statistics and some insight. But the Negro, in his role as a private person, does not talk frankly to a strange white man, or even to one he knows well if there is even a vestige of the old master-servant relationship. He may, and most often does, mask his feelings in an almost excessive politeness, but unhappy experience has long since taught him not to freely offer his trust across the color line.

It was my extraordinary good fortune to come, through mutual friends, upon James Booker, political writer and columnist for Harlem's *Amsterdam News*. Jim Booker tendered me courtesies and services far beyond the normal call of duty of the journalistic underground, as did his wife, Jean, who lightened some of our long evenings with the pleasure of her company. In the course of journeys that took us into the murky corners of most of New York's scattered Negro communities, Booker proved to be not only a first-class journalist but a first-class human being. He did this, in a way that is especially relevant, by neither accepting my view nor attempting to impose his upon me—an achievement I find unique in a relationship that seems to produce an emotional compulsion among both whites and Negroes to instruct others in their own version of revealed truth about the inner nature of the problem.

It follows, then, that while this book would have been impossible without Jim Booker's assistance, he bears no responsibility for its findings and conclusions. I can only hope that there is some repayment for the considerable debt I owe him in the memories we share. I know his wry amusement matched mine on the Saturday night we went down to Greenwich Village to observe the interracial rites of the Beatniks, those untidy representatives of his race and mine who, out of sloth and rebellion, have taken up residence in a sort of subcellar of society. We had been duly warned away from the tourist traps and provided with the presumed address of an authentic pad, but it turned out to be as elusive as a floating crap game. In a quiet turning we came upon a dimly lit basement restaurant with well-draped windows and went inside, only to be firmly barred beyond view of the customers by a hatcheck girl, eventually backed, in the face of our importuning, by a large man in a dinner coat. He was sorry, but all tables were taken, and no, the crush was such that it would not even be possible for us to stand at the bar. At the moment I decided to concede defeat Booker moved around in front of me, shoved his dark face forward, and gently inquired, "Are you refusing to serve *me* a drink?" There was a silence, during which the bouncer considered the possible consequences of an investigation by the New York State Commission Against Discrimination, and we were ushered inside what turned to be only a standard Village resort for homosexuals.

Any undertaking of this kind is beset by the hazard of wounded sensibilities. The truth about the condition of our Negro people is unpleasant, and to many members of both races intolerable; the mere recitation of the facts can topple a whole structure of cherished rationalizations. This produces the kind of selective reading that was sometimes reflected in the considerable volume of mail attracted by the newspaper series. A white matron in Columbia, South Carolina, found irrefutable proof that the ungrateful Negroes have finally taken over the government and wanted to know what is to become of us all. A Negro social worker in Chicago read condescension into the most straightforward passages of reporting, and concluded that the whole thing was a malicious and misbegotten effort at humor. And, to add to the awkwardness of the sanitized vocabulary already required for nonoffensive usage, I am informed by the Committee to Present the Truth About the Name "Negro" that the only really acceptable term is Afroamerican.

These reactions are symptomatic of deep-seated fears They sometimes make effective communication between on one side and deep-seated grievances on the other.

the races impossible, and contribute measurably to the difficulty of resolving the most durable social problem of our time. Yet they too are part of the reality, and must be faced. The South tried to translate prejudice into law, and has found the effort doomed. The North tried to pretend that prejudice didn't exist, and for too many years looked the other way while the racial ghettos grew and festered. In both regions the issue has been consigned, by default, to moralists, when realists are desperately needed.

I entertain the hope that this condition is changing, along with everything else that effectively has to do with the practical relationship between whites and Negroes. The tensions and dislocations of these critical years may well mark the transition from one era to another. If their abrasive effect cuts away some of the myths and shibboleths we have lived by, we may yet discern that truth which we were long ago promised would make us free— white and black alike.

THE OTHER SIDE OF JORDAN

CHAPTER 1

THE EDGE OF
BITTERNESS

HARLEM'S favorite joke these days goes like this: Two colored maids are rattling uptown on the subway at the end of the day's work. One is telling the other about her new job.

"They're fine folks to work for, and it sure is interesting. They entertain a lot and know all the important people. Why, just last night for dinner we had Vice-President Nixon, Adlai Stevenson, Governor Rockefeller, Senator Lyndon Johnson, Mayor Wagner, Mrs. Roosevelt, Dag Hammarskjold, Clare Boothe Luce, Chief Justice Warren, Helen Hayes, Carl Sandburg, and Robert Frost."

"Sure enough? When big people like that are just among themselves, what do they talk about?"

"Us."

This pointed fable has currency not only in uptown Manhattan, but in all the swarming big-city ghettos for which Harlem stands as a symbol. In its sly way it says a lot about the fermenting mood of America's colored minority—and about the increasing concern and perplexity of the white majority.

The response it evokes still reflects the rich humor of a people who have learned in adversity that laughter can be a saving grace. But there is an edge of bitterness, too.

In the Red Rooster, where Harlem's intelligentsia exchange the latest word, a light-skinned man—middle-class in dress, manner, and speech—hears the joke and adds his own footnote:

"Well, they've got a lot to talk about—and not much time left for talking."

Across the street from the Rooster, behind the weathered charcoal-gray walls of the Abyssinian Baptist Church, the nation's most spectacular Negro spokesman offers a self-serving variation on the theme.

In the austere auditorium, Adam Clayton Powell stands before a strangely-wrought brass cross presented by the Lion of Judah, Haile Selassie, facing a primly starched Sunday afternoon congregation come to protest the latest atrocities in the Union of South Africa. The handsome preacher-politician spreads his arms and intones:

"I came back from the Bandung Conference in 1955— five years ago—and I went to the White House and I told

Mr. Eisenhower the shape of the future. 'Mr. President,' I said, 'I have been there and I have seen and I have heard. And I say to you, Mr. President, this is the truth America must recognize if we are to survive: The timetable of freedom is no longer in the white man's hands!' "

The response from the audience is a rising, muted sigh. (You do not shout and holler in a proper Negro church these days.) And one has the feeling that Congressman Powell once again has struck the right chord, and in return these good and earnest people are prepared to wash away their pastor's numerous sins.

At the corner of Seventh Avenue and 125th Street, when the weather is right, you can hear the voice of Negro protest in its harshest accents. Here the patient policemen stand by while the street-corner orators mount their stepladders and use their braying loudspeakers to preach the gospel of Black Nationalism, at home no less than abroad. The tone and, remarkably, most of the vocabulary, are those of a White Citizens' Council rally in a Deep Southern town.

The targets are white politicians and businessmen, the "lying newspapers," the "phony liberals and the bleeding hearts and the do-gooders," and even the National Association for the Advancement of Colored People, which at this far end of the oratorical spectrum stands as a conservative organization.

Here, naked and undisguised, you come upon what—

if it were not for the intricacies of the Negro attitude—
would have to be written down as anti-Semitism.

A young man in a white trench-coat leans into his microphone and shouts: "The Jew-dominated NAACP is no
friend of yours!" A dozen of the faithful in the front row
shout back: "That's right!" Beyond them, silent and
thoughtful, stand a hundred or so more who have paused
in their routine passage down the broad sidewalk. Change
the skin color, make a few minor alterations in the script,
and you can shift the scene intact to Heflin, Alabama.

These sights and sounds do not, of course, reflect the
total mood of the Negro community. In many and probably in most cases they are contrived and manipulated by
a horde of colored con men who, like their white Southern counterparts, have discovered that it is possible to
make a living out of exploiting a people's anguish and
resentment.

The litany at Seventh and 125th is not new. Forty years
ago the founder of Black Nationalism, Marcus Garvey,
paraded through these streets under a banner bearing a
black star, proclaiming separatism for the Negro people
and calling for a march back to Africa. In the 1930's the
corner was inhabited by a man from Philadelphia who
called himself Sufi Abdul Hamid and sported a beard, a
turban, a green velvet blouse, a Sam Browne belt, patent-
leather boots, and a red-lined cape. Sufi, too, preached

Buy Black, Boycott White—and honed an edge of anti-Semitism against Harlem's Jewish landlords and store-keepers.

The slogans of Negro protest that sound now from St. Augustine to San Francisco have been heard before—but what is new is the fact that no Negro leader of conse-quence can any longer afford to ignore them. Now the crude harangue of the charlatan echoes the drumbeat of revolt in Africa and the sustained resistance movement of Negro college students in the American South. These things are no longer emotionally separable.

The NAACP, the Urban League, most educators, and the ministers of conservative churches still stand against the extremists, but with increasing caution. Negro politi-cians try to avoid formal identification with the Muslims, the African Nationalists, the Garveyites, and the various offshoot groups, but their public stance rarely advances beyond neutrality. The militants have forced some pre-viously critical Negro newspapers into silence, or even active support, by the open threat of boycott.

Here, as in the white South, the advocates and the devotees of extreme action are no more than a tiny mi-nority of the total population. But the loud voice, and the threat of a concerted move by a disciplined group, has its effect. So, too, and perhaps more importantly, does the emotional response aroused in even the most conserva-tive Negro by an unabashed cry for vengeance against the whites who are the authors of his real and fancied grievances.

"I know as well as you do," says a suave Negro publicist, "that the Muslims and the others are talking nonsense when they talk about boycotting the whites and creating a separate Negro state in this country. I know these movements are small and filled up with crackpots and phonies, and that in the end they won't get anywhere. But when they give the white man hell every Negro likes to hear it."

These are far from being the elements of revolution, but they do portend change—social, political, and economic change to fit the still unrecognized facts of the vast redistribution of Negro population within the United States.

The great migration from the South is not yet over, but it has already reached the point where the headlines that record the dramatic final assault on the crumbling walls of Southern segregation are little more than a historical footnote.

In the second half of the Twentieth Century the American Negro is seeking his future—and increasingly will insist upon shaping it on his own terms—in the great cities. As long ago as 1956 the advertising trade magazine, *Printer's Ink*, published a list of metropolitan Negro populations ranked by size; it ran through eight cities before it recorded a single one in the South proper: New York—1,045,512; Chicago—605,346; Philadelphia—484,644; De-

troit—357,800; Washington—337,757; Los Angeles—276,-
305; Baltimore—226,661; St. Louis—215,336; Birmingham—208,705. The continuing migration of the last four
years has increased the non-Southern concentrations by
an average of 15 to 20 per cent, and in some places the
rate of growth is even more spectacular. From 1950 to
1957 New York recorded an increase of 42.5 per cent in
its nonwhite population; current estimates are that the
Negro community in Los Angeles exceeds half a million,
and is the third largest in the country. Comparisons by
percentage of total population are even more revealing;
a 1960 estimate prepared by the Library of Congress
showed Washington as the only large American city in
which colored population has passed the halfway point to
55 per cent. This compares with the highest Southern
concentration of 40 per cent, in Jackson, Mississippi.

These are urban people, and the patterns of the agrarian
past fit neither their needs nor their aspirations. In the
course of the long journey upward from slavery, they
have put down old burdens, but they have found new
grievances.

The outlines of the future are far from clear. But in
the big-city ghettos, in the churches and the bars, the
schoolrooms and the smoky political clubs, the festering
tenements and the shabby-neat apartments of the new
middle class, there are clearly audible sounds that can
only mark the end of an era.

These portents have not been lost on the established Negro leadership, although they appear to have come as something of a shock to some of the more complacent occupants of high places. White leaders, however, still seem to have some difficulty deciphering the message. In many ways one of the most astonishing public utterances of the century was President Eisenhower's bland pronouncement that any real improvement in the relationship between the races would have to await a change in the minds and hearts of men—and this reiterated even after he had been forced to the virtually unprecedented act of sending federal troops to occupy the streets of an American city caught in the travail of racial disorder. The first fact of contemporary life is that no Negro leader, no matter how temperate his personal persuasion, can any longer accept the president's proposition and maintain a position of authority or prestige in his own community. Theodore H. White has written perceptively of the Negro politician "picking his way through a tangle of pressures within his domain and without" and has warned: "He can remain master of his coalition, and keep it just this side of violence, only so long as he gets from white politicians and delivers to his voters their full fair share."

In the past many Negroes whose individual capacity gained for them a degree of acceptance by whites and resulting status in the larger community have tended to drift away from the difficulties and occasional pain of active participation in Negro affairs. I recall a conversation reflecting the melancholy of a gray afternoon that cast a special pall over Harlem's grim streets. My companion was a Negro professional man who had attained prosperity and general public recognition in the course of a career that had taken him downtown in successful competition with his white colleagues.

"My wife and I have been making plans for retirement," he said. "I've still got a good many active years ahead, but our only child is in college now and will soon be leaving home. In a year or so I'll be eligible for a pension that will give us enough for a comfortable living. I've about decided to quit and get out of Harlem.

"For the last few years we have been spending our vacations in Puerto Rico and the Virgin Islands. It has been a revelation to both of us—being in places where there is no color bar and where there never has been one. In most of the communities down there color simply doesn't matter, one way or the other; it just isn't relevant. That's what a white man really can't understand, how it is even here in New York where under the best of circumstances a Negro always has to be conscious of being different. I'm not one of those who goes around with a chip on his shoulder, and these days I'm treated pretty well anywhere I go. But you can never be sure when you walk into a strange place whether you're really going to be welcome, and even if you are the people on the other

side are likely to overdo it, and that can be just as un-
comfortable.

"In the Islands there's none of that. I hadn't realized
it before, but I guess I never have been really relaxed
since I've been grown. My wife and I have about made
up our minds that as soon as we can we'll buy a house
and move down for good."

Over the years this sort of emotional withdrawal has
cost the Negro community much of its potential leadership. But these days white and Negro universities are
pouring forth an increasing number of colored graduates
to swell the once thin ranks of the professional class, and
experience in the integrated armed services is endowing
many other Negroes with new skills and poise. These
youngsters tend to scorn the conservatism and human
weariness of their elders, and there is no reason to expect
this rising tide of talent to diminish or change its course.
Although their capacities are as yet largely untried, these
will be the architects of the new era—not radicals in the
classic sense, but men and women clearly endowed with
the driving force of impatience.

CHAPTER 2

THE WAY
OF LIFE

NEGROES like to repeat the old saw that is presumed to explain the difference between the North and South: In the South the white man doesn't care how close a black man gets so long as he doesn't get too high; in the North the white man doesn't care how high he gets so long as he doesn't get too close.

It retains an element of truth. The white man who lives outside the South doesn't really see the Negro if he can help it; and when he can't help it, he is likely to be irritated and alarmed. Nowadays the word *Negro* flashes in the back of his mind accompanied by another—*Problem*.

The growing colored communities in the heart of the great cities and on their industrial fringes are beyond the white man's orbit.

Once they were thought of as exotic, and sophisticated

whites made pilgrimages there as they would to a tropical country. In the Twenties and Thirties Harlem was the fashionable last stop for a night on the town in New York. Anita O'Day used to sing:

> If it's pleasure you're about,
> And you feel like steppin' out,
> All you've got to do is shout:
> Let me off Uptown.

Uptown then was the Cotton Club and the Savoy, and a dozen glittering supper clubs where the prohibition law and the closing ordinances could be bent for a price. It was a place where Satchmo blew his golden horn, and high-yellow girls strutted under blue spotlights, and old Bo-jangles tapped out his wonderful, loose-limbed message on the hardwood staircase.

Today the white tourist trade is long gone. In all of present-day Harlem there are perhaps six or seven night spots that still provide live music, and this the product of obscure combos that attract no more than a handful of the far-out music set. A night club still bears the name of Count Basie, but the Count doesn't play there any more; like all the other great Negro musicians he has gone down-town to the expensive white resorts. And in the increasingly open city of New York the Negro jazz aficionados can follow the cats; if they've got the price, a ringside table is available to colored people, too, at Birdland and Eddie Condon's and the Embers.

So there is no reason for the white man to go into Harlem any more, and he sees it only from the commuter's train window, and usually hears of it only in newspaper headlines that tell of crime and corruption, and in the somber statistics composed by sociologists.

A passing glimpse from the elevated tracks of the New York Central does tell something of the story. There is misery and squalor behind the streaked tenement windows; swarms of yelling, pink-heeled children do run untended in the garbage-strewn streets; at night a dim street light does pick up the slumped form of a wino or a junkie propped against the wall of a dingy neighborhood bar.

And it is true that the bright, red skein of violence runs through the varied fabric of community life in Harlem, and every other big-city Negro ghetto.

Accurate figures on Negro crime are not easy to come by. In New York and other cities, in response to pressure from the NAACP and allied agencies, most public criminal records no longer carry racial identification. Newspapers, responding to the same pressures, generally avoid the racial tag in their crime reports. The humane objective is to avoid overemphasizing the incidence of Negro crime; after all, it is argued, Italians, Irish, Jews, Poles, and even WASPS (white, Anglo-Saxon Protestants), also commit crimes and are not so identified. The result of the policy is often the reverse of the intent—to reinforce the exaggerated fears of those whites who attribute virtually all crime to Negroes and Puerto Ricans and assume that the Negro neighborhoods are lawless jungles.

An FBI report which attempted to summarize the matter showed that in 1,551 cities Negroes, who make up about 10 per cent of the total American population, accounted for about 30 per cent of all arrests, and 60 per cent of arrests for crimes involving violence or threat of bodily harm.

In 1958, *Time* magazine, revealing in its breathless way what it termed a "shocking pattern," offered this rundown based on the probing of its correspondents:

New York (14 per cent Negro): Of the prisoners confined in houses of detention to await court disposition of their cases, 44 per cent of the males and 65 per cent of the females were Negroes.

Chicago (15 per cent Negro): In 1956 twice as many Negroes as whites—1,366 to 679—were arrested on charges of murder, non-negligent manslaughter, rape, and robbery.

Detroit (25 per cent Negro): Two out of three prisoners held in the Wayne County jail were Negroes; in 1957, of 25,216 arrests resulting in prosecution, excluding traffic cases, Negroes accounted for 12,919.

Los Angeles (13 per cent Negro): In 1956 Negroes

accounted for 28 per cent of all arrests, and 48 per cent of the arrests for homicide, rape, aggravated assault, robbery, burglary, larceny, and auto theft.

San Francisco (7 per cent Negro): The victims of 896 of 1,564 recorded robbery cases in 1957 reported that the assailants were Negroes.

Lurid though they may be, the details are not really important. There is Negro crime, a great deal of it, and of all varieties from the relatively innocent peddling of numbers tickets to the brutal mugging of unwary after-dark pedestrians in Central Park.

The existence of the Negro ghettos poses special problems for the big-city police. There is, at one end, the protective sensitivity of the Negro people who tend to fear the law and to refuse to cooperate in routine enforcement. At the other end there is the ghetto's corrupting influence on the police themselves. Some succumb to the ready temptation to go on the take in return for ignoring petty gambling and vice; others give in to the human tendency to take out the frustrations of uniformed life on the poor black devil who can't fight back—and thereby contribute some facts to the lurid tales of police brutality which occupy so much space in Negro newspapers.

In New York, Police Commissioner Stephen Kennedy has approached the problem in two ways. In the sensitive areas, white and Negro policemen usually work in teams, and the commands are regularly shuffled in the effort to deliver the officers from temptation. On top of this there is a trouble-shooting force of "Commando Cops"—all six-footers with special judo training in handling mobs by hand, without recourse to the firearms which are always likely to ignite the fuse of a tense situation.

Even so, the Commissioner's troubles go on. Scandal has repeatedly rocked his department. He has had to face the highly embarrassing disclosure that for a price it was possible to have the official records in the Central Identification Bureau altered so that a ten-time loser among the numbers runners would appear before the judge as a first offender. A numbers runner, of course, is by definition a Negro, and so the fix was presumed to begin in the colored neighborhoods—although it is a reasonable assumption that it was actually arranged and paid for by the white gangsters who run the lottery racket and take off most of the profits.

At the other end, even the Commando Cops have had their troubles in the rougher Negro neighborhoods. In the Bedford-Stuyvesant area of Brooklyn, probably the toughest spot in all New York, a hostile crowd of 500 poured into the streets after a stray bullet killed a delivery boy, and the police officials who handled the emergency situation reported that only the grace of God averted a riot. A few days later one of the Commandos was mobbed and mauled in the course of a routine arrest of a Negro on complaint of his wife.

At its most alarming, the crime pattern reflects the cutting edge of Negro bitterness against whites—a senseless, compulsive striking back against oppression, real and fancied, and against authority, which for the Negro equates with a white skin. It is a curious fact that the growing number of Negro policemen have no automatic immunity in this regard; for the harried and resentful, the blue uniform is the mark of the enemy no matter who wears it.

But seen in any perspective, it is clear that this is only a minor part of the problem, and not in fact a growing part. The sociologists can demonstrate from the record that crime is an inevitable product of the American ghetto, whatever the pigmentation of its residents. Wherever there is human misery, and little hope for a cure, there emerges a pattern of broken homes and untended children, and in the end a kind of sullen revolt not only against the law but against the conventions of society.

The Rev. Joseph P. Fitzpatrick, S.J., a Fordham sociologist, speaking in defense of the Puerto Ricans, who have reacted to the same slum conditions with a special Spanish fervor, quotes with pointed irony from the writings of John Pintard, a New York charity reformer of the 1830's:

. . . the beastly vice of drunkenness among the lower laboring classes is growing to a frightful excess, owing to the cheapness of spirits and the multitudes of low, Irish Catholics who, restrained by poverty in their own country from free indulgence, run riot in this. . . . As long as we are overwhelmed by Irish immigrants, so long will the evil abound . . . thefts, incendiaries, murders which prevail, all arise from this source.

But there is a great deal more to the Negro communities than the symptoms of violence which disturb the untutored white. There are, in Harlem, quiet streets where on a warm night you may come upon a pipe-smoking Negro in Bermuda shorts peacefully walking his dog. Sugar Hill, the one-time haven of colored show people and athletes who had reached the big time, still has a fading glory about it, and there are apartment-house doormen there, and limousines for them to tend.

Harlem, in fact, has most of the hallmarks of a self-contained small town, but one that stays up later than most. The private local vocabulary includes a reference to C.P.T.—Colored People's Time—which runs an hour or two behind that in effect downtown. Few of the bars anticipate New York's legal 4 a.m. closing time, and even the sedate private entertainment of the bridge-playing set is likely to continue far past midnight.

There are, of course, dark turnings into which a man wearing an air of prosperity and a little gone in liquor would proceed only at his peril—but if he were rolled, an objective investigation would probably reveal that it was done without particular malice, and without regard to race, creed, or color.

In the brightly lighted commercial areas, where the ordinary humdrum business of life goes on, a man with a white skin has no difficulty making innocent passage. If he is looking for trouble he can probably find it, and wind up carved like a Thanksgiving turkey. But if he minds his own business he will be treated with courtesy and respect—the special, almost painful politeness that any close-knit community reserves for the identifiable stranger in town.

Even on a hot Saturday night, in the places a proper middle-class Harlemite would call "blood-and-guts joints," and assiduously avoid, a stray white man encounters no special feeling of tension. The impression is not one of unrepressed hilarity and unleashed inhibitions. Rather it is one of slow, wearing misery. The long line at the bar, knocking back the 30-cent "doubles" which in fact are thick-walled shot glasses containing a one-ounce dose of the cheapest blended whiskey, is made up of men and women who seem to be trying to get through the long night and reach oblivion.

There are still visible signs of the Old South, incongruous here against the background of brownstone-row houses and old apartment buildings marked by the cracked marble of departed elegance. There are still restaurants bearing crudely hand-lettered signs advertising "chitterlings with two vegetables, 90 cents," or "pogies and whities, 75 cents." The store-front preachers are still around, shouting salvation as they used to do in Montgomery, or Charleston, or Memphis. Even on 125th street, above the neon-lit, plastic-coated chain stores where the busy week-end shoppers pass in and out, second-floor windows silhouette the writhing forms of young girls and old, lumpy women far gone in the religious ecstasies of a soul-saving conducted in the name of the late Daddy Grace.

You can find almost anything in Harlem, if you look: decent sober people trying to make out against the odds and sometimes succeeding; innocents from the back country or the Caribbean islands who will never understand the meaning of the great city whose towers loom beyond the park; and those who, either inherently crippled or maimed by circumstance, have slipped over the edge of the great social abyss of our time.

You can find in the ghettos almost anything but happiness. The bluebird nests somewhere else.

CHAPTER 3

THE
NEW ISLAM

LENOX AVENUE and 116th Street was once the main corner of the Harlem that Carl Van Vechten, in a simpler time, without offense could identify as "Nigger Heaven." It isn't an important intersection any longer, but it still embraces a sagging office building bedecked by signs that are intended to signalize the American Negro's protest movement.

A white man entering the old building causes a mild flurry. An ancient custodian peers out of his cubbyhole with obvious surprise, and a numbers runner scuttles off down the street to spread the word of possible trouble.

The open-cage elevator ceased functioning in some forgotten epoch. Worn, dimly lighted steps take the visitor upward across the yawning distances between old-fashioned high ceilings, and past closed doors that recite their own pathetic litany.

The second floor is the headquarters of the Garvey Club, keeping alive the name of old Marcus, the first and probably the most spectacular of the Black Nationalists. On the third floor there is the Universal African Nationalist Movement, a splinter of the larger United African Nationalists which is the private preserve of a smooth-talking public-relations man named James R. Lawson. Down the hall a door bears the impress of the Prophet Judah. The fourth floor is taken up with a sizable meeting hall which is Temple Number Seven of Muhammad's Islam—the New York center of the so-called Black Muslim movement which now makes militant anti-white sounds in every major city of the country.

All these doors are firmly closed to the white visitor. So are the meetings of the Muslims, where even those with black skins must submit to search upon entry. There is the unmistakable aura here of the secret society—and one who has lived in the South thinks instantly of the ironic parallel with the Ku Klux Klan.

The Muslim movement began, so its reluctant historians say, about twenty years ago in Detroit. The major temple is now in Chicago, and this is the seat of the aging, bald man who came into the world as Elijah Poole and now calls himself Messenger Elijah Muhammad. The claims made on behalf of the Messenger in his own publication go like this:

Messenger Elijah Muhammad, spiritual leader of America's Muslims, whose undisputed control of his fast-growing, well-disciplined, fearless young followers . . . and his growing influence throughout the African-Asian world, makes him one of the most loved and respected Black Men in America. He heads the best organized group of young Black people in the Western hemisphere, dedicated young people whose 'unto the death' obedience of his fearless and uncompromising leadership amazes and impresses his sharpest critics.

There is the sound of bugles here, and of a call to arms, and it follows that the Messenger's sharpest critics include the police officials of a number of cities, who keep a wary eye on the movement. In Los Angeles, where the Muslim invasion is fairly recent, Chief Parker has asked in the public interest that the local newspapers not publicize it, and they have complied.

Muhammad does not see white newspapermen, but on occasion his number two man will. He is the prophet of the New York temple and the editor of the sporadic Muslim publications—a thin, tense man of medium color who was christened Malcolm Little, the son of a Baptist preacher, and who will say of his youth only that he "grew up all over." Today he calls himself Malcolm X, rejecting his pre-Muslim surname as the unworthy heritage of a white man who thrust it upon a slave forebear.

Malcolm insists that the Black Muslim movement is an authentic offshoot of Islam; the Messenger, he says, has made the pilgrimage to the inner shrine at Mecca, and the only reason he hasn't gone himself is that he didn't want to get there ahead of his ecclesiastical superior. This claim is privately and somewhat indignantly denied by practicing Middle-Eastern Moslems in this country, but there has been no official disclaimer because there seems to be no one to provide it in a religious movement which operates without a priesthood and relies largely upon the individual's inner call.

In any event the Black Muslims are unshakable in their assertion that theirs is, among other things, a religious movement. Those who join must sever their ties with other churches. They are enjoined to follow the Moslem dietary proscriptions against pork and alcohol—and for good measure the Messenger on his own motion has added tobacco to the list. Malcolm says the faithful eat only one meal a day, and face East to say their prayers. Cosmetics and fancy clothing are frowned upon; a hot bath every twenty-four hours is mandatory; and the male members normally shave their heads. Malcolm wears the somber black hat and suit, and the stiff white collar and black tie of the conventional Protestant minister.

Franklin Williams, former NAACP director on the West Coast and now assistant attorney general of California, has said of the movement: "It combines the emotional religious drive of Father Divine and Daddy Grace with the legal and political protest of the NAACP, and on top of that it offers the hope of a Black Utopia on this earth. Above all, it gives the poor, ignorant, disturbed Negro a sense of identity—something the white world has always denied him. This is its appeal, and it is a powerful one."

The Muslims preach brotherhood, but it is restricted to the Blacks. (They reject the term Negro, and refuse to use it.) The white man is at worst an enemy, and at best a neutral. Malcolm claims that he can produce two hundred of the faithful on any street corner in Harlem within five minutes if there is a racial incident worthy of Muslim attention. What would they do? "Whatever is necessary," Malcolm says, "but peaceably, of course. We do not start trouble. But we do not turn the other cheek."

Most visible Muslim activity consists of picketing—to protest what the Muslims consider white discrimination, or to push the economic line that Negroes should spend their money only with Negroes. This is the pie in the sky, and its most tangible evidence can be seen in Chicago, where the Muslims operate their own school (for children mostly, but proudly called the University of Islam), grocery stores, restaurants, garment-manufacturing plants, and a rudimentary department store. This, proclaims the Messenger, is the harbinger of the American Negro's future—a completely separate and self-sufficient Black community which will not have to depend upon the white man for capital, services, or employment.

Malcolm takes the dream to its ultimate absurdity.

"Marcus Garvey was right as far as he went," he says, "but he was wrong in telling Negroes they should go back to Africa to achieve their goal. We're going to build our own society here in the United States. We're going to have our own all-Black state."

Malcolm's vision is a complete entity, with its own government and, presumably, with an official connection or at least diplomatic relations with the United States. Where would he locate it? He is not specific, but he summarily rejects the ironic suggestion of a Negro reporter that there might be a good many people in the country who would be willing to give him Mississippi.

Malcolm shows no sign of being aware that what he and the Messenger are really preaching is the basic segregationist doctrine of the Southern White Citizens' Councils—and, to add the ultimate touch of irony, the separatist policy that in the Twenties and Thirties was part of the American Communist Party line. There is a strange, intense innocence in this man, who freely talks about his own conversion to the Muslim faith during the seven bleak years he endured in a Massachusetts prison after being convicted of breaking and entering in the nighttime.

Malcolm himself still does a considerable amount of recruiting for the movement in the local jails.

"Prisons are all corrupt, you know," he says, out of the wisdom of experience. "If you've got the price you can get anything in jail—cigarettes, liquor, even dope. We think a man ought to be able to get the true religion in jail too, and we try to provide it. Most of the prison officials won't recognize us as a religious group, and I have been denied visiting privileges in some places. But we've got converts in all the major prisons. And when those prisoners come out they'll be wonderful additions to our movement. Cowards don't go to jail, you know. We'll rehabilitate these men and women and they will march in the ranks."

There are, of course, no available membership figures on the Muslim movement. Even as does the Kleagle of the Klan, Malcolm only grins wisely and says, "We're big and we're growing."

Muslim literature lists the main centers as Chicago, Detroit, Boston, Pittsburgh, Newark, Los Angeles, and New York, but there are small groups active now even in many of the Southern cities. The symbolic use of X as a last name (the first John to join is John X, the second is John X2, etc.) serves as a public mark of identification, and can be used as an instrument of pressure. Thus when advertisements start appearing in Negro newspapers identifying the advertisers as John and Mary X, the publisher can assume that a Muslim leader will soon be around to discuss editorial policy. The Muslims have leaned hard on the *Pittsburgh Courier*, which circulates nationally, and on New York's *Amsterdam News* and the *Los Angeles Herald American*.

"It is interesting," says Malcolm, who also edits the sporadic Muslim rotogravure magazine, "that while the *Courier* carried a column by Mr. Muhammad, the circulation went up. When we discontinued the column the circulation went down."

Whatever the reason, the Negro press now generally treats the Muslim movement seriously, and in its usual sensational way probably gives it a certain added impetus.

Even so it is doubtful that any of the Temples, with the possible exception of Chicago's, could count an actual membership of more than a thousand. Only the most heavily promoted Muslim rallies attract an attendance in excess of that figure, and it must be assumed that the audiences are padded by curiosity seekers, colored newspaper reporters, and undercover agents of the police.

But even a few fanatics can make a fairly loud noise, and the Muslims have discovered another truth—that it is part of the white man's racial myopia that to him a couple of dozen colored men look like a crowd, and possibly even the beginning of a mob.

Riding in tandem with the Muslim movement are the United African Nationalists. But, while the Muslims retreat from the white world to make their incantations, the

Nationalist operation is of necessity entirely public. There could be no greater contrast than that between Malcolm X, with his professed and apparently genuine asceticism, and the unabashedly sybaritic James R. Lawson. Lawson's expensive clothes hang smoothly on his well-padded frame, and he looks entirely natural holding court as he leans against the bar in Harlem's most elegant restaurant.

Lawson makes no effort to conceal the fact that he wears two hats—one as head of the Nationalists, and the other as a member of a Harlem public-relations firm. In candor, he even concedes that in some important ways the two roles overlap, as in the case of certain accounts obtained from the governments of newly emerging African nations. But candor disappears when he is pressed as to the exact nature of his duties for these foreign clients.

Whatever their purpose, his Nationalists are primarily street-corner orators. They, too, urge the boycott of white merchants, and more pointedly than any of the others press an anti-Semitic line. Ralph Bunche of the United Nations, the senior statesman of American Negroes, recalls a low inside curve pitched at him by Lawson in the course of an introduction at a Harlem rally. This consisted of a heavily sarcastic reference to Bunche as "the George Washington of Israel." The veteran diplomat countered with an equally pointed reminder that he had spent as much time in Cairo as he had in Tel Aviv.

Lawson has a way of turning up in the public company of visiting African dignitaries, and has become a hard man to ignore. Thus Africa Freedom Day, which is something of a private Lawson promotion, now has the sanction of a mayoral proclamation. In advance of its last observance Lawson announced a gigantic rally at Seventh Avenue and 125th Street and promised crowd-drawing addresses by Adam Clayton Powell and Hulan Jack. The police dutifully turned out in force under the command of a deputy-inspector, and marked out an entire block with their saw-horses. But Powell and Jack never appeared, and sent only the most perfunctory regrets. Lawson blandly explained to the reporters from the New York dailies that there apparently had been some confusion, and took to the microphone to salvage what he could by urging that the spectators buy copies of his white-baiting Nationalist newspaper.

Curiously enough, such a fiasco as this seems to have no more effect on Lawson's status in the community than it does on his brass-plated aplomb. He remains a personage, and one to be reckoned with. This may result in part from his own nerve and skill, but it seems to be primarily due to the potency of the cause to which he has attached himself.

The Muslim and Nationalist symbols of that cause range from the pathetic to the ludicrous, and the movement clearly is not going anywhere—not, certainly, toward practical achievement of the separate black state proclaimed as its goal. But if the hot-eyed Malcolm X and the suave James Lawson chart no coherent course they nevertheless reflect the fact that the mass of Negro people are no longer willing to stand still.

CHAPTER 4

PROFILE
OF POVERTY

IT IS NOT an easy thing to be Robert William Daniels
of 325 Lenox Avenue, Harlem.

If you live at that address it is a foregone conclusion
that you inhabit a dark skin. Daniels' is medium brown,
his wife's is even darker, and the shading runs off toward
dusty blue-black among the ten children and one grandchild who make up the Daniels family.

This small horde lives in five tiny rooms, strung together
shotgun style, on the third floor of a creaking building that
surely is ticketed to go down one of these days before the
bulldozers of slum clearance.

It is a place where cockroaches run, and rats, where
the garbage moulders in halls pocked with old obscenities
carved by forgotten residents, and where the shrill voices
of angry tenants echo, unheeded, through the night.

It is not, by a long shot, the worst tenement in Harlem. But it will do as a symbol of the poverty that even in an age of abundance still blights much of the area.

It is the only home Daniels and his growing family have known since the founders and the firstborn came to New York from Macon, Georgia, fifteen years ago. Robert William was twenty-four then. His wife, by his estimate, was fifteen, but she insists primly that she was sixteen when he sent back for her. Over the years the mathematics of this union have doubtless confused the numerous social workers who have trudged up the steep and cluttered stairs—but the evidence of its success is unmistakably there in the persons of the remarkably healthy and composed children who play quietly in the cluttered rooms even while strangers are being entertained.

The Danielses receive guests, after supper at least, under something of a disadvantage. The two adults, when I called, were horizontal, propped up in bed before a television set which had attracted a predictable quota of the younger children. There was only room for two plastic-covered chairs in the narrow space between the double bed and the bleached-oak bedroom furniture which lines the walls.

There was no need to explain this informal arrangement. Coming into the apartment from the rear you pass the tiny kitchen with its utilitarian equipment. From there on the rooms are understandably filled with beds.

"One of the things I hate about this place," Mrs. Daniels says, "is, a man comes home from work and takes off his pants and there is no place to hang them. No closets, no place even to throw them down. All you can do, you just eat and go to bed, and maybe look at the television."

"It's bad," Robert William agrees, "but I reckon I don't mind it as much as Pat does. She stays cooped up here all day, and I get out, and that makes it easier."

When he goes out Robert William proceeds three blocks to the Harlem office building he tends as superintendent. Firing the furnace, cleaning the halls, and hustling a few odd jobs for the colored tenants brings in an income that never exceeds $250 a month and often falls well below. In times past the Danielses have been intermittently on the welfare rolls, but theirs is a borderline case. Besides, Mrs. Daniels doesn't like the social workers.

"They come in here and they want to know how we can afford the telephone, and who paid for the good bedroom furniture, and I tell them my sister-in-law is keeping up the payments and they don't believe me," she says with a snort of disgust. "If we can make do without the welfare, we do."

"I manage to keep them fed and dressed decent and in school," Robert William says with a wave at the circle of dark young faces looking solemnly in from the next bedroom, which is without a shielding door. "It's the housing that's so bad, having to live all huddled up like this. I'm still trying but I haven't licked that."

The big problem is the very size of his family. It has practically barred him from low-rent public housing, which rigidly limits per-room occupancy and rarely provides apartments big enough to accommodate a family of thirteen, with more doubtless to come.

"I have walked my feets off going to the projects," Mrs. Daniels says. "I just get a lot of talk, and then I have to come back and live like this. I declare if it keeps up I'm going to have a nervous breakdown."

"She won't, though," Robert William says fondly. "She talk like that, but she strong. Somehow we going to make it. I got a feeling the break is coming."

It is difficult to see where it is coming from. Robert William obviously can't afford more than the $35 he now pays in monthly rental—and he has all the private housing that that sum will buy in Harlem. At thirty-nine, his income would seem to be limited permanently by his lack of any real skill.

He's a big man, and a husky one, and those who know him say he works hard. But schooling ended for him in Macon at the sixth grade, and he learned nothing more than use of his muscles when he worked as a helper in the yards of the Central of Georgia railroad.

"I wasn't getting anywhere, just leveling the coal on the tenders and things like that, and so when my father-in-law came back from New York and said he could get me a job up here I decided to come," he says. That job was as superintendent of the building in which he still lives. It became the only trade he has followed since he joined the great northward migration.

The move from Macon, then, hasn't improved the physical environment of the Danielses. Their tenement is one of those once described by Thomas Sancton as "a hundred Delta cabins, plus tuberculosis." And plus the incessant noise, crowding, confusion, and hazard of big city streets.

Why did they come?

Robert William is not an articulate man, and he finds it hard to explain.

"Well, the chance of a better job, of improving myself," he says. "It's not much better, but the chance is here. And freedom, I guess—knowing if I got in trouble the law wouldn't always be against me. And feeling like a man. You can't do that in the South, they just won't let you."

"Lord, yes," Mrs. Daniels chimes in. "I went back to Macon last year to bury my mother, and they all walking around crying the blues. We wouldn't go back to stay, not ever."

"But mostly for the children," Robert William says, gazing upon his brood with gentle eyes. "It's hard for them to grow up here, but if you look after them and treat them strict they can make it. All mine have stayed out of bad trouble.

"Hard as it was, I never would let Pat take a job when

they were real little. After the biggest girl got old enough to stay home and look after the others, Pat would go out and take domestic work sometimes. That's when we got the phone—so if anything happened somebody would call her or me."

The things that can happen to a Harlem slum child are, of course, legion. But Robert William thinks things are getting better.

"I've lived right here for fifteen years, and I've seen the changes. There are more parks, and playgrounds in the housing projects, and more space around the schools. And when they tear down some of these old buildings and thin the people out it helps. Used to be there was fighting all the time in the streets. I've seen men dead on the sidewalk right under these windows. You don't see much of that any more, and you don't hear the loud cussing, and the whores don't strut around like they used to.

"There's still the wineheads and the junkies. Seems like as many get hooked as ever did, and they just walk around dying with it and they can't quit. I see a lot of the young men go that way, and it's just like they trying to kill themselves. But you know, it's a funny thing, they usually kind to children, and they come and tell me or Pat when they see one of our young ones going somewhere he shouldn't. That's when I crack down.

"I remember when the big boy tried to start smoking. That was when he was thirteen or like that, and I grabbed him and said don't you forget I'm your daddy and you may have had more schooling than I did but I've lived longer and I'm bigger than you are and if I catch you with a cigarette I'll knock it down your throat."

He's not bigger any more. At nineteen, Robert William, Jr., has shot up to six feet two, and one of the family dreams is that the basketball prowess he displayed at Commerce High will yet bring him a college scholarship. His picture, in his graduation cap and gown, stands on the oak dresser as something of a shrine.

The boy is working now as a messenger in a wholesale liquor firm, saving his money, and going to night school to make up the credits he will need for college. In September the Danielses hope to be seeing him off to Howard University, the old Negro institution in Washington. If he makes it, he wants to study pharmacy.

The oldest girl, the deserted mother of the grandchild, is taking a secretarial course. The other children stair-step down through the grades of public school.

If these plans succeed, the children will move out of the closed Negro world in which their parents live and will likely die. The orbit of the elders is wholly within the ghetto; the crowded tenement, the office building where Robert William works, the Baptist church where they worship, the neighborhood bars in which he buys an occasional shot of cheap whiskey. The rare family excursion is across the river to Paterson, New Jersey, to visit cousins who also made the pilgrimage from Macon.

In the course of his days, Robert William has few contacts with whites and displays little personal animosity toward them. They run the world that presents his immediate, endless, and consuming problems of food and clothing and shelter, but they are abstractions beyond his ken.

The Negro protest movement does not seem to have touched him except in a remote, emotional way.

"I hear about those kids in the sit-ins down South," he says, "and I'm proud of them. And I hear a lot of talk about what's going on over there in Africa.

"I listen to the politicians talk about these things, and I try to read up on what's going on, but it doesn't seem to change anything. I've been to see the district leader I don't know how many times about getting in the projects, but all I get is promises and we still living here all huddled up. It's the same way with the NAACP and the Urban League—just more talk.

"I vote all right, sometimes Democrat and sometimes Republican, and sometimes the split ticket. Pat here, she don't even bother, hasn't voted but once since we left Georgia."

Like the older generation of Negroes in the South that sired him, Robert William tends to put his final reliance in God.

"I'm a religious man, and I've raised my children to be

religious. We go to church, and we go to pray, not to socialize like a lot of people do. I believe in the Golden Rule and I try to live by it. I don't do nobody no harm if I can help it, and I try to forgive those that do me harm. A man can use himself up just hating. I got faith—that's why I know the break is finally coming."

Mrs. Daniels interrupts this testament with a petulant toss of her head in its old-fashioned stocking cap. "He got more faith than I have," she says. "I tired of waiting."

"Ain't nothing to do but wait," Robert William says gently. "Wait and hope and pray. If the break miss us, it surely coming for the children."

It will come, if it does, in ways that Robert William can hardly envision, for these children, with their father's innocent blessing, will be sent out into the white world which long ago closed out him and his kind.

But one thing is certain. None of the Danielses, old or young, will be heading back to Georgia.

CHAPTER 5

THE PLACES
OF POWER

N O ONE WOULD ever mistake J. Raymond Jones for anything but a politician, and a successful one. He has the look—the gray hair shading now into white, the subdued and impeccably neat clothing, the easy manner and sense of presence that comes of sitting frequently at head tables. He smokes cigars, naturally, and they come from Havana. His drink, in which he indulges sparingly, is an esoteric brand of Scotch for which bartenders have to search in the bottom shelves. His conversation is rich in personal anecdote, and laced with earthy humor.

Had he been born Irish, or Italian, he might well have been the leader of Tammany Hall by now. As it is, he was born Negro, in the Virgin Islands sixty years ago, and so he has only made it as far as membership on Tammany's executive committee.

You don't have to talk to Ray Jones long before you understand why Harlem long ago nicknamed him "The Fox." Like all big-city politicians, he has been in and out. He was first elected to the leadership of Harlem's key 13th Assembly District in 1944. His star rose with that of Mayor William O'Dwyer; he became deputy commissioner in the Department of Housing and Buildings and headed Tammany's powerful rules committee.

At one time, he says, O'Dwyer talked seriously about making him leader of Tammany despite his dark skin. How did he respond?

"I wasn't interested," he says. "You will note that Bill O'Dwyer is not around any more, and I still am."

Even so, Ray Jones also had his years of political eclipse —beginning in 1952 when he resigned his district leadership and settled for a quiet patronage job as secretary to a General Sessions judge. In 1958, he came back upon the scene under a standard bearing the strange device of Adam Clayton Powell.

Powell had departed the Democratic reservation in 1956 to campaign for President Eisenhower. In 1958 he came home again to campaign for Averell Harriman. The circumstances of this round-trip excursion have been the subject of much speculation; a former Powell aide, Fred Weaver, has charged that it took a campaign contribution of $50,000 to get Powell over to the Republicans, and a contribution of $100,000 by the Democrats to get him back.

"Certain financial arrangements have to be made to pay the legitimate cost of any campaign," says Ray Jones of these matters. "I can only say that in my experience the actual figures are usually exaggerated by the time they appear in print."

Jones managed Powell's inevitably successful campaign for re-election to Congress in 1958, and was himself returned to his old district leadership. The liaison with the mercurial Congressman has stood up since, which in itself is noteworthy, since Powell has left a trail of disgruntled former associates strewn from one end of Manhattan to the other. Currently Jones is credited with swinging the deal that brought together the two old foes, Powell and Borough President Hulan Jack, and at one point in the process tossed a set of Puerto Rican leaders and candidates out the back of the sleigh.

True to his breed of politician, Jones is not interested in issues but in results. In his view the Powell-Jack United Harlem Leadership Team—which is also and perhaps appropriately called the Axis—is the natural product of the present New York political situation, which finds Tammany under attack by an insurgent Democratic group and Carmine De Sapio's hand visibly shaky on the tiller.

"Put Jack's and Powell's groups together and we swing 20 per cent of the votes in Manhattan," Jones explains.

"Swing those votes right and we ought to wind up with 20 per cent of the jobs. If we do that we don't need the Puerto Ricans—and anyway the break with them makes Carmine nervous, and that's good for us."

Whether this formula will survive the intricacies of the city-wide struggle for Democratic power, and the pressures of a presidential campaign year, remains to be seen. Shortly after its inception the Axis was set back in one major maneuver by the reinstatement of the once-dismissed malfeasance indictment against Jack, and the hung jury which sidetracked the anticipated acquittal of Powell in his sensational income-tax case. In the face of all this, Jones at the last minute had to abandon his effort to get Tammany's endorsement for a judgeship for Jack's lawyer, Carson Baker. He failed, too, in a remarkable attempt to persuade the executive committee to give the endorsement to a Negro judge already nominated by the Republicans. In the end, Jones had the support only of his six-member Negro bloc and the nomination went, in immemorial fashion, to meet the formula patronage demands of New York's Jews.

This, however, is only part of the game. Jones remains unshaken in his confidence that De Sapio is heading for his last vote-roundup.

"When the leaders run again, Carmine is done," he says. "I plan to be around to help pick up the pieces. I've seen control of this town pass from the Irish to the Italians.

Anybody who can count votes ought to be able to figure out that the Negro's turn is coming—if not for control, at least for a bigger share of the pot."

Ray Jones, too, is perhaps an inevitable product of the shifting patterns of urban life. He has his counterpart in every big city where Negroes have concentrated in numbers. He exists, and performs in the old manner, simply because Negroes make up the last real bloc vote left in the land.

There are still measurable remnants of the older ethnic and religious minorities that left their imprint on American politics—the Jews, the Irish, the Germans, the Poles and the Italians. But these are gone from the ghettos now for the most part and in their passage into suburbia and the middle-class they have tended to lose their special identity and often to consciously reject it. This is the process that has cost the Democrats so heavily, and has given President Eisenhower his towering majorities. One mark of respectability, after all, is membership in the Republican Party.

Men like Jones, then, have a vested interest in keeping the Negro ghettos intact, and he makes no bones about it. Of the effort by the American Civil Liberties Union to have the Census Bureau drop all racial identification, he says:

"Silliest damned thing I ever heard of. How am I going

to bargain for the Negroes if I can't prove where they are? I'm losing too many as it is, with all this crossing over the color line."

The patterns of Negro political action vary with the circumstances of the cities. In Detroit the Negro bloc, so far, has swung with the CIO leadership, and has even been diverted to the support of white congressional candidates running against Negroes. In Chicago the veteran Negro congressman, William Dawson, runs his show along conservative and traditional patronage lines, parlaying the small wards in the Black Belt into six seats on the City Council.

The concentration of Negro votes in clearly defined areas has now sent four Negroes to Congress—Dawson, Powell, Charles C. Diggs, Jr. of Detroit, and Robert N. C. Nix of Philadelphia. James Q. Wilson, who has made perhaps the most complete current analysis of Negro voting strength, figures Negroes are due to cast the majority vote in eight more congressional districts in the near future unless there is extensive gerrymandering—two in California, and two more each in Illinois, Michigan, and New York. On state and local governing bodies, elected and appointed, Negroes are increasingly taking their place.

The political strength of the Negro bloc has not, of course, gone unchallenged. In Los Angeles, where the City Council redraws its district lines every four years, it somehow has fallen out that the Negro vote has remained a minority in any given district—with the result that with 276,000 Negroes in the city, and probably twice that in the county, Los Angeles has only one colored officeholder of consequence, State Assemblyman Augustus Hawkins. In Cincinnati, when a prominent Negro lawyer, Ted Berry, ascended to the post of vice-mayor, the old system of proportional representation, which favored the solid bloc vote, was abandoned. Berry, who previously had run second, dropped to fifteenth in a field of eighteen.

Negro leaders themselves are divided on the question of using the Negro bloc vote to carve out certain direct Negro benefits. To do so does, of course, accept the present segregated communities and tends to perpetuate them. In theory, at least, it is almost the reverse of integration, which has long been the professed goal of national Negro spokesmen.

To Ray Jones this argument is nonsense.

"A lot of our people listen too much to sociologists," he says, with the old political pro's typical scorn. "Sure, the white liberal leaders in the past have done a lot of things that needed doing. But why did they support anti-discrimination laws and public housing and all the rest? Because the Negro vote has been growing steadily and they couldn't ignore it. I say it has grown big enough so that Negroes can take over their own show. We're not leaving our old friends, we're just tending to our own business."

It is in the nature of the precinct politician to maintain

only a perfunctory interest in national politics. In the case of the Negro bosses this is likely to be overlaid with an undisguised cynicism. They know any candidate they back must make obeisance to federal civil rights legislation, and that in presidential elections this continuing issue is used by many Negro voters as a sort of litmus test to determine who is worthy of their support. But they also know that eight years of President Eisenhower's inertia on civil rights on one hand, and the resistance of the Southern Democrats on the other, has blurred any real distinction between the two parties and their national candidates. In times past, when the issue was clearly drawn, or seemed to be, a single properly-timed campaign speech could send an emotional surge through Harlem that could be translated into votes not only there but in Negro communities across the nation. This was done by Harry Truman in 1948, and by Adlai Stevenson in 1952; no one, however, can readily visualize either Jack Kennedy or Richard Nixon setting the political woods on fire with the traditional bid for Negro support from the balcony of Harlem's Theresa Hotel. The party platform planks on civil rights amount to a standoff, and if Nixon has an edge in personal popularity among Negroes it is too slight to be a determinant.

Normally the urban Negro vote splits with a heavy majority on the Democratic side. This is a heritage from the New Deal days, bolstered by the fact that in most of the cities the Democratic precinct organizations have access to local patronage and are far better organized than their Republican competitors. Barring the diversion of an emotional upheaval, the Democratic captains are generally able to deliver the votes in ratios that run as high as five to one, a concentration that can be a significant factor in a close election. Republican inroads into these majorities in 1956 were probably due to popular Negro disillusionment over what they thought was Stevenson's softening of his racial line between elections, plus the lassitude of many Negro bosses left in the wake of the bitter convention break between the Stevenson and Truman-Harriman factions. Even so, the Republicans actually carried few Negro precincts; Adam Clayton Powell's campaigning for Eisenhower, after his carefully staged conversion on the White House steps, didn't swing his own Congressional district into the Republican column.

Still, the Negro vote is a prize that commands much effort on the part of both parties. And because effort in politics means the expenditure of considerable sums of money there are always Negro politicians around to encourage even the most unlikely contender. Months ahead of the 1960 Democratic convention a Harlem district politician who, as is so often the case, is also a public relations man, was openly boasting that he had a deal with the Lyndon Johnson people.

In his 1958 gubernatorial campaign against Averell

Harriman, Nelson Rockefeller superimposed a high-geared special task force on the local Republican organization. It was headed by a ubiquitous former citizen of Harlem who has been living for ten years in, of all places, Arkansas —James Hudson, the colored manager of Winthrop Rockefeller's multi-million-dollar cattle ranch. Hudson's presence in Harlem over a period of months was in part the result of a strategy decision by Rockefeller's managers. He was there to serve as a living rebuttal if Harriman tried to make capital out of brother Winthrop's official association with Orval Faubus as chairman of the Arkansas Industrial Development Commission; here was a Negro who not only held executive position in a Rockefeller enterprise, but served as the boss of a large group of white workers in a Southern state. There was another reason, too. Without rancor, Harold C. Burton, Harlem's veteran Republican leader, says of Hudson's activities: "I expected him, or somebody else closely associated with the Rockefeller family. It has been my experience over the years that when a Rockefeller starts spending money in politics he puts one of his own in charge of the purse strings."

In the politics of the Negro ghettos the quick deal and the fast shuffle are a way of life—if not more so than elsewhere in the practical conduct of the cruel game, more openly admitted and candidly defended.

"What else have we got to work with?" bluntly asks

Ray Jones. "Sure, our people can get worked up over the civil rights issue. But what we need are jobs and houses and street lights. You get those by dealing for them.

"A presidential candidate who would really take a stand on civil rights—who would get up and say, and mean it, that he was going to use all the power of the federal government to end discrimination against Negroes once and for all—a candidate like that could carry the Negro vote all over the country, and blow us practical politicians right out of the tub if we didn't go along with him. But who's going to do it, in this election or any other election in my lifetime? Nobody. As for me, I'll settle for a politician I can do business with. I'd be happy with Lyndon Johnson—and I didn't mind saying so when we put him on the ticket at Los Angeles."

Even so pragmatic a formula, however, depends in large measure on the men out front—the advocates who take the case to the Negro people, and find it necessary to dress it up with an appeal that stirs the emotions. In his own drive for increased Negro influence in Democratic affairs, there can be no doubt that Jones has chosen to back an able and fast-paced political contender.

Adam Clayton Powell is touched with both genius and charm. There are few better orators abroad in the land, and the content of even his most florid effusions reflects the genuine erudition of the graduate of Colgate and Columbia. When he cares to work at it—which isn't often—few politicians do a better person-to-person job in the sweaty political halls with the hearty handshake and the remembered name.

Starting with the base of 11,000 inherited members of his late father's Abyssinian Baptist Church, Powell has carved out an impervious political domain for himself. To do this he has relied primarily on a Negro nationalist line —with overtones taken from the African revolution— which his critics, including the leaders of the NAACP, have denounced as racist extremism. But the emotional response it arouses among Negroes of all classes is his shield and buckler against all suspected personal wrongdoing—even as segregation is Orval Faubus'.

The Negro precinct politicians accept Powell because they have no choice, but they neither admire nor trust him. Jones is hardly in position to offer a candid personal appraisal of his candidate, but it doubtless would not differ greatly from that of Burton, who briefly had Powell in his Republican camp after the big switch in 1956.

"I still like Adam," Burton says. "It's hard not to like him. He'll cut your throat if it suits his convenience, and the truth is not always in him. But with all of that, there really isn't any malice in the fellow. Sometimes I think that may be part of the problem—that he just doesn't really care enough about anything, except Adam Clayton Powell."

It is not even certain that Powell has the usual politician's drive for power. The influence he has acquired so far he has used mainly to guarantee his personal pleasures, which are expensive—Upmann cigars, Napoleon Brandy, a midtown suite in an expensive hotel, frequent trips to the European watering spots, a beach house in Puerto Rico. He moves around New York with an entourage like an old-fashioned gangster's or a television comedian's— press agents, check-payers, door-openers, coat-holders, telephone-answerers, and several remarkably pretty girls.

These things the Negro people have given Powell. So far he has given them little in return, except perhaps hope, which is not an inconsiderable commodity. The real test in the years ahead will turn on the ability of the Ray Joneses in the back rooms to parlay this simple faith into the reality of jobs, housing, and civic betterment.

CHAPTER 6

THE REVOLT
IN LABOR

PRESIDENT George Meany of the AFL-CIO exploded into headlines early in 1960 with the announcement that he was prepared to take a group of non-union electricians by the hand and lead them onto a union job in Washington—an offer as remarkable as any ever made in the history of American organized labor.

Had Meany not simmered down before he carried out his threat, the hand-led electricians would have been Negroes. The immediate object of the old plumber's wrath was lily-white Local 26 of the International Brotherhood of Electrical Workers, which in this instance was keeping colored electricians from working on a Federal office building, even as it and its brother craft union locals had barred Negroes from employment on one of the very citadels of the integration movement, the palatial Washington headquarters of the AFL-CIO itself.

Meany's scatterload penetrated a number of sensitive skins—including that of Vice President Nixon, who heads the Government Contracts Committee with the mission of seeing that no contractor who accepts federal payments practices racial discrimination in employment. The incident, however, was thoroughly bi-partisan. Another victim was Matthew McCloskey, the prime contractor, who also happens to be the national treasurer of the Democratic Party. Mr. McCloskey could only explain that he had offered to bring down Negro electricians from Philadelphia but that Local 26 had threatened to strike if he did—and that the Vice-President's committee didn't think this was the answer anyway.

Whatever the final answer may be to the problem posed by Local 26, and those like it that exist in every major city in the country, it is evident that the leaders of the union movement are still a long way from finding it. More than a year before his spectacular public outburst Meany had issued a direct order to the president of the IBEW to open Local 26 to Negro membership, and had set October 31, 1959, as a deadline for compliance. His order was ignored.

In the meantime Meany is being needled from the rear, and the needle is in the expert hands of one of the elder statesmen of national Negro leadership—A. Philip Randolph, president of the Brotherhood of Sleeping Car Porters and a vice-president of AFL-CIO. On the open floor of the 1959 AFL-CIO convention in San Francisco the old porter sent the old plumber into another eruption in the course of a debate dealing with discrimination in various member unions.

"Who the hell appointed you the guardian of all the Negro union members in America?" Meany shouted at Randolph.

Whether duly appointed or not, Randolph has now formally assumed the role. In May of 1960 he convened the founding convention of the Negro American Labor Council in Detroit, giving substance to a paper organization which for some months before had maintained headquarters in the old Harlem building that houses the Porters' Union.

"Our purpose is clear and simple," Randolph says. "We're going to use the collective power of the million and a half Negro union members in this country to end racial discrimination within the unions wherever it exists —and it exists in plenty of places."

Richard Parrish, the young firebrand who serves as secretary of the new Council, has stated the goal even more forcefully before the New York Labor Forum, a somewhat intellectual group made up of union educational directors and the like.

"You might as well get used to the idea," he told his visibly disturbed audience. "We're going to raise unmitigated hell inside the labor movement, and outside it too, if that becomes necessary."

In that effort the new Council has had the open, if initially reluctant support of the National Association for the Advancement of Colored People. Herbert Hill, the NAACP's national labor secretary and, incidentally, one of the last whites to hold a major position with the organization, shared the program at the Labor Forum with Parrish and more than matched his fervor.

Hill's device was to call the roll of virtually every major union in the country, craft or industrial, and cite examples of discrimination against Negroes ranging from absolute bars to Negro apprenticeship, through Jim Crow locals, to the failure of even the open unions to give Negroes proper recognition in policy-making positions.

"And mark it down that I'm not talking about locals in Atlanta and Memphis and Little Rock," he thundered. "I'm talking about locals in Pittsburgh and Philadelphia and Cleveland and Detroit and right here in New York. I'm talking about locals in places where the union leaders talk loudest and longest about civil rights.

"When you were out at the AFL-CIO convention in San Francisco, did you know that in the heart of that great liberal city you couldn't buy a drink from a Negro union bartender? Well, the California FEPC was then investigating the case of Ray Bass, who had been trying to crack the all-white local for a year, and couldn't get a job in a desirable location because they wouldn't accept him."

It was a stinging report on union apprenticeship restrictions drafted by Hill and given wide general publicity that marked the first break between the leaders of the NAACP and the CIO-AFL, who had marched together for years under the common banner of civil rights. Dick Bruner has reported in *The Nation* that Executive Director Roy Wilkins of the NAACP tried hard to settle the issue behind the scenes. A memorandum on union discrimination was submitted to Meany with the suggestion that a word of assurance from him might temper or resolve the conflict. Meany sent back a perfunctory reply in which he said he could offer no such assurance, and Hill was unleashed.

In the matter of apprenticeship, Hill charges that the old craft unions of the AFL are the greatest offenders—as indeed they always have been—with the building trades and the railway brotherhoods at the head of the list. Here the Negro not only faces race prejudice but becomes entangled in the restrictive practices by which apprenticeship programs are often sharply limited and the training period stretched over years. Since this is the only means of entry into the craft union locals, a Negro who can't penetrate the curtain is simply denied the opportunity of skilled employment in a city where these unions hold tight control—as they do in most.

The complaints against the industrial unions of the CIO

are on a different level, but they are only slightly less acute. Even the United Auto Workers, considered the most open of all unions and headed by labor's most consistent and articulate champion of civil rights, Walter Reuther, does not escape the fire of Randolph's new council. One out of every eight members of UAW, it is pointed out, is a Negro, but only one out of every seventeen UAW staff personnel is colored. Moreover, some Negro staff workers are there only for protective coloration in a public-relations sense, and are given no real authority.

Only six of the AFL-CIO unions have Negroes in positions of elected leadership. They are Randolph's virtually all-Negro Brotherhood of Sleeping Car Porters, the United Packinghouse Workers, the Hotel and Restaurant Workers, the Allied Industrial Workers, the International Longshoremen's Association, and the National Maritime Union. Although Negroes and Puerto Ricans are increasingly numerous in the needle trades, the traditional liberalism of the garment unions has produced no significant break in the controlling Jewish hierarchy.

When Hill and Parrish recited these charges before the Labor Forum they drew an almost anguished rebuttal. No speaker from the floor successfully challenged any of the specifics, but all in one fashion or another raised two points—the fact that the unions traditionally had fought for welfare and civil-rights programs of special benefit to Negroes, and the fear that an open battle within the ranks along color lines would divide and weaken the entire union movement.

The reply of Hill and Parrish in effect was that of the constituent who interrupted his political boss' recitation of past favors with: "But what have you done for me lately?" And Hill concluded with a threat of further action on still another front. "Don't be surprised," he said, "if you find yourselves meeting us in court."

Randolph, turned seventy now and rich with memories, is more philosophical than his young associates, but no less keen for what may be the last great battle of his long career. He can remember others when the danger was personal and immediate.

"I used to go into the South when you had to hide out to have a union meeting, even if it was segregated. You weren't even safe in a church. I've been in Memphis when Boss Crump's police would come right up to the pulpit and give the order for the organizers to be out of town before the sun set. You knew they meant it, too.

"But you know, in some ways it was easier then than now. There were tough old fellows in the AFL in the South in those days who would stand up and fight for us and run real risks. Most of them, I guess, believed in segregation just as much as Boss Crump did, but the issue was simple justice and they understood that and they'd fight for it.

"What we're up against now is something different. Oh, there is still race prejudice in the unions, sure. But on top of that there is the fact that whites have always run most of the unions, and if we are going to move up on the inside it means somebody has got to move over. Nobody ever likes that."

He recounts a conversation with a Negro auto worker in Detroit who had entered a union election for shop steward. The old steward came to his opponent, with tears in his eyes, to ask what he had done wrong. Hadn't he worked over the years to open jobs for Negroes, and hadn't he always gone out of his way to be fair when they did get on? "You know," the colored candidate told Randolph, "I never could make him understand that he hadn't done anything wrong, that he had been fair, and that we all liked him and were grateful to him, but that I just thought it was my turn for the job."

Any realistic appraisal of the labor patterns in the country will sustain Randolph's contention that Negroes are bound to attain greater influence in many unions by sheer weight of numbers. In common labor and the service and needle trades there is no longer a family progression; the sons of the hodcarrier, the waiter, and the garment-maker are likely to move, with their fathers' blessing, into a trade or profession that offers greater material rewards, or, perhaps more importantly, a higher social status. The replacements increasingly are Negroes and Puerto Ricans.

Randolph is not at all impressed by the argument that he is threatening the whole of the labor movement by his effort to marshal these new forces against the established leadership.

"Nobody has said anything yet about our new Council that I haven't heard before," he says. "They used to say the AFL was tearing the labor movement apart, and Lewis' mine workers, and the CIO. Yes, I've heard it all— and I've seen the labor movement grow strong on internal conflict.

"But there is more to it than that. The basic philosophy of the trade union movement is to bring an end to discrimination—not just economic discrimination but any kind of treatment that demeans the working man. Of course, we've never entirely practiced what we preached. My own union is still segregated except for a few white workers on the Canadian lines. It started that way because it was the only way it could start. Do you realize that as late as the 1930's our 35,000 members accounted for almost half the total number of Negroes in the AFL?

"But that time has run out. We've got to fight now to get our full rights within the unions, and not only in justice to our own people. I say that what really weakens the union movement is its own practices of discrimination; as long as that goes on we are disarmed before our enemies.

"And there's another, maybe a bigger reason."

In the Saturday afternoon quiet of his dingy office,

looking down on the teeming streets of Harlem, the old man tells of being literally taken off a train in North Carolina by a delegation of Negro college students who found out his traveling schedule and came aboard unannounced at an operating stop.

"They scared the life out of the porter, and he tried to keep them out. I think he even told them I wasn't on the train but they knew better, and they just pushed him backward into my compartment. He kept saying, 'For the Lord's sake, Boss, don't go with these people. They're wild.'

"But they told me they had a car waiting, and they needed me on their campus, and they would take me on to Charlotte to meet my appointments. It was the sit-ins they wanted to talk about, of course. They already had them going in two of the North Carolina cities and they were planning more.

"So I went with them, and when we got there the whole auditorium was full of students and they had been waiting for hours. The president and some of the faculty came in to greet me, and they looked pretty nervous, and I guess I couldn't blame them. That whole place was full of electricity. You could feel it.

"I got up to talk to them, and when I looked out over those young faces there wasn't but one thing I could say. I told them I would do what I could to help. That's what I'm doing now—trying to help the best way I know how."

CHAPTER 7

THE UNEASY
NEIGHBORS

A SOUND-TRUCK pulls up to a corner on upper Madison Avenue. A handsome, dark-suited man climbs to the top, picks up a microphone, and sprays the gathering crowd with a hail of Spanish.

He is Luis Ferré, and he is, of course, running for public office—but not for an office in the city of New York or even in the continental United States. He is the Republican-Statehood Party candidate for governor of Puerto Rico.

For a week Ferré took his sound-truck through Spanish Harlem, the Bronx and Brooklyn, pausing along the way to kiss babies (who are remarkably abundant in these precincts) and hand out his campaign literature. Earlier, his Democratic opponent, the incumbent Governor Luis Muñoz Marín, was in town on a similar mission.

These political visitations were prompted by a statistic that might astound New Yorkers, many of whom feel they are being engulfed by a rising tide of volatile migrants from the United States' commonwealth in the Caribbean. The Migration Division of the Puerto Rican Department of Labor figures that 29,989 Puerto Ricans came to the mainland in 1959. Ferré calculates that just about that many will go back to the island this year. These are the voters he is appealing to in New York; he assumes that after they have stayed in the States a while they will be disposed to support his campaign for full statehood.

Ferré's admonitions to his street-corner audiences say a good deal about the nature of the newest of New York's newcomers.

"You must learn English," he tells them. "You must get over your inferiority complex, and learning English will help you."

But at the same time he insists that, while he stands foursquare for political assimilation through statehood, the Puerto Ricans must avoid "cultural assimilation." Here again is a politician with his eye on a bloc vote.

When they first began swarming into New York after World War II, the Puerto Ricans were usually officially classified as nonwhite. They are often still so regarded by many whites, who tend to think of them as somewhat eccentric Negroes. However, under Puerto Rican protest the official identification has now been abandoned.

The fact is that Puerto Ricans have little in common with Negroes except the same problems of poverty, housing, employment, and general discrimination. Probably no more than 30 per cent of them are dark-skinned enough to pass unnoticed in a Negro bar. In culture and temperament they are as separate from the Negro community as they are from the white.

Although many of them live cheek by jowl with Negroes in the ghettos there is virtually no social mixing—and there is often a great deal of tension. There has been relative quiet on this front lately, but some of the worst of the juvenile gang rumbles of a few years ago involved Puerto Ricans versus Negroes.

So far the force of circumstances has kept most Negroes and Puerto Ricans physically together. In the early days of their arrival the islanders actually served in effect as skirmishers for the Negro community in its struggle for housing and for jobs. Light-skinned Puerto Ricans would be accepted in fringe neighborhoods where Negroes were barred. When they sent back to the island for their families, some dark members inevitably would be included in the next contingent. With the line broken, the Negroes moved in behind them; this is how Harlem was extended down both sides of Central Park. The same thing was true in employment, and the pattern is not confined to New York.

"There is a Puerto Rican community of about 3,000 in

Milwaukee now," says Joseph Monserrat, director of the Puerto Rican Department of Labor's operations in the United States. "It was founded a few years ago when we got a request for a number of laborers from a foundry out there. The first ones we brought in were light-skinned and the white workers accepted them without protest. The next batch included some darker men, but they spoke Spanish and somehow this protected them against the usual prejudice. After that it was simple for Negroes to take their place in the work lines, and in the confusion they gained acceptance before anybody was quite sure what had happened."

Milwaukee's 3,000 Puerto Ricans are not, of course, all a single foundry's workers and their families.

"The immigration simply began in a single plant, and under our control. To protect our people against exploitation we do not allow labor recruiting in the island. Requests have to be cleared through us, and we see to it that the workers get the going wage and are protected against discrimination. We do not, for example, accept requests for farm workers from the Southern states, although we get a good many. This sort of controlled immigration still accounts for a good part of the total—but we are a free people and there are many others who come on their own. Puerto Rican families are close-knit, and when a new arrival finds a place he sends back for his children, his parents, and sometimes his cousins and his aunts. And they'll spread out wherever there are job vacancies."

Puerto Ricans have been classified as American citizens since 1917, and therefore are immune to immigration quotas. The reason the great influx did not get under way until the 1940's, Monserrat says, is purely economic. He has a chart in which the peaks and valleys of immigration closely follow the curve of U.S. national income.

In the Depression Thirties there was actually a decline in Puerto Rican population, as the lack of jobs forced many back to the island. In the booming postwar years of industrial expansion there was a vacuum at the bottom of the United States labor market—in the service and garment trades and for common labor—and Puerto Ricans and Southern Negroes flooded into the great cities to fill it.

New York initially got the bulk of the Caribbean newcomers, and is still the port of entry for most. Monserrat's guess is that there are presently about 800,000 Puerto Ricans in the United States, with slightly less than 700,000 concentrated in the boroughs of Manhattan (289,000), Bronx (173,000), Brooklyn (179,000), and Queens (12,000).

New Jersey and Connecticut industrial cities in the New York area have acquired sizable concentrations; in 1958 Bridgeport could count 10,000, Hartford 4,500, and Newark 13,000. In other areas the big concentrations are in Chicago, which had 25,000 in 1957, and Philadelphia, which had 20,000 in 1958, with another 5,000 across the river in Camden.

Every Puerto Rican community is growing, but primarily by birth now. Monserrat's immigration figures show a decline from the 1953 high of 69,124 to 29,989 in 1959. The future pattern, he believes, depends upon the economy; continued improvement in conditions in Puerto Rico will tend to keep workers at home, and any shrinkage in the mainland job market would force them to stay there.

"But don't expect the magnet of economic improvement to disappear," Monserrat warns. The island is crowded, about twelve times as densely populated as the mainland, and the birth rate is high. With all the internal advances of recent years, the average family income is still about $500 a year, as against the mainland's lowest, $1,500 in Mississippi. Opportunity still lies to the North.

These figures explain the miserable conditions the Puerto Ricans have endured in their first years in the New York ghettos. Unscrupulous landlords quickly discovered their willingness to pack into tenements under crowded conditions Negroes would not accept without protest—and thereby were able to turn a fast dollar by renting a family a room instead of an apartment. But it has worked another way, too. Because their prior living standard was so low, Puerto Ricans have generally saved money out of even the bottom-scale wages initially available to them. This has enabled them to open or take over an impressive number of small neighborhood businesses—far more, proportionately, than Negroes have acquired in the far longer period they have occupied New York's slums.

Two of Harlem's leading Negro business men, Hope Stevens of the United Mutual Insurance Company, and Joseph E. Davis of the Carver Federal Savings & Loan Association confirm this trend and anticipate its continuance.

"I'm not sure they are more frugal by nature than Negroes, but their savings accounts here are impressive, and they are excellent loan risks," Davis says. "Of course they have a natural advantage in setting up those neighborhood businesses. The new arrivals speak only Spanish and they want to go where they understand what is going on and can protect themselves. Then, in general, they are a more clannish people—held together by their religion and their different ways. The Negro doesn't have any of those drives; he just wants to live as well as he can and he trades wherever he can get what he wants."

How long that clannishness will survive under the pressure of urban living is a matter of conjecture. The Puerto Rican's inherited identification with the Catholic Church does not seem to be particularly durable, and the Irish and Italian-oriented Church in New York only in recent years has undertaken much in the way of special ministry, charitable services, or even parochial schooling for these imported children of the faith. Many have drifted away to join the flocks of the Pentecostal hellfire-and-brimstone preachers, and the local Spanish-language newspapers regularly carry advertisements listing Episcopal, Evangelical, Methodist, and Presbyterian services as well as those of the Catholic churches. Presently the Church in New York is attempting to counter this trend with a policy under which a substantial number of the priests and nuns graduating from its seminaries are assigned to temporary service in Puerto Rico and required to master Spanish. But a telling measure of the trend away from Catholicism lies in the fact that a heavy majority of Puerto Rican children are being educated outside the church; in 1959 they made up 15 per cent of New York's public school pupils, a proportion comparable to that provided by the predominantly Protestant Negro population.

Spanish continues as the common language of the Puerto Rican neighborhoods, clung to in many cases in a deliberate effort to maintain a special mark of identification that separates the islanders from Negroes. But all the newcomers quickly master a working command of English on their jobs, and the children absorb the new tongue in the normal course of schooling. Within a relatively few years it should be possible for any light-skinned Puerto Rican who wants to do so to disappear in the conglomerate population of the big cities.

Some are already breaking out of the ghettos and entering New York's scattered middle-class.

"Go out to Levittown," Monserrat says, "and you'll find a good many families living there that nobody even thinks of as Puerto Rican. They're blue-eyed and fair-skinned and they talk and dress like the neighbors—and worry about the same things."

All the signs indicate that the difference in pigmentation will make the upward journey for the Puerto Ricans far easier than it has been, or will be, for the Negroes who now share the New York slums with them. This is a source of special Negro resentment—perhaps a far more active source than the occasional direct competition with Puerto Ricans in the labor market.

"How do you expect me to feel?" asks a Harlem newspaperman. "If I am arrested I go on the working police records as Negro or nonwhite. A Puerto Rican as dark as I am is listed as white. And don't think it doesn't make a difference—at least as long as they're not looking at you."

The Puerto Rican is still below the Negro in the social pecking order of newcomers, and in political influence. But he may not be there too much longer to peck at.

It was in part the practical maneuvering of New York city politics that led not long ago to a midtown Puerto Rican rally in which the flow of Spanish from the speakers' platform was broken occasionally by the words "Adam Clayton Powell" and "Hulan Jack"—and greeted by a chorus of boos. The next day in the Renaissance Ballroom, Powell and Jack launched their United Harlem Leadership Team and announced that Puerto Ricans had been dropped from their ticket. The rift was later patched up after a fashion, but it seems likely that the politicians were simply confirming a historic development that had already taken place.

CHAPTER 8

PROFILE
OF PLENTY

CROSS THE line from the Bronx and your first stop
is Mount Vernon in Westchester, which thinks of
itself as the wealthiest county in the world, and
may be.

Mount Vernon's 70,000 souls now fill its four square
miles of territory, and are heir to all the problems known
to a suburban satellite clinging to the edge of a great city.

One of these is race. The best guess is that the Negro
population is now running around 17 per cent, and the
new census figures may well raise that figure.

Many of these Negroes have been there twenty years
and more. Some of the first came as domestic servants for
the local bedroom community of middle-class New York
commuters, and for the estates of the big rich further up
the Hudson. Others were attracted by jobs in Mount Ver-

non's fringe of garment factories and light industries. A substantial number commute across the river to industrial jobs on the Jersey side.

In the nature of the Negro migration these working-class families long since were consigned to their own local ghetto, and have filled it with a solid black front. They occupy the older, least-desirable housing, and have been able to expand their neighborhood at the edges without particular strain as white families have moved away under the natural process of improving fortunes. There is even a district of Negro cafés, bars, barber shops, and small stores on the edge of the main business section.

The ghetto, of course, has posed some problems for Mount Vernon, but they seem to have been handled reasonably well by the conservative, Republican burghers who maintain firm control of local affairs. There is no particular sense of racial strain in Mount Vernon, not, at least, in the sections down along the railroad tracks.

In recent years, however, Mount Vernon has been subjected to a new Negro invasion—small in numbers but high in potential social significance. These are people of substantial income and above average educational attainment who themselves are fleeing the blight of the big-city colored neighborhoods. They seek to climb the hills beyond the railroad tracks and find a place along the tree-shaded streets where a generation and more of white families—Jewish, Italian, Irish, and assorted Protestant—

have found a quiet backwater away from the clamorous metropolis.

Officially, Mount Vernon has welcomed these professional and business-class Negroes and there has been no overt act of discrimination. When a rock crashed through the living-room window of a newly arrived Negro physician a few years ago the mayor announced that this sort of thing would not be tolerated in his town, and the police launched a relentless investigation that quickly tracked down the culprit. He turned out to be a teen-ager guilty not of racial prejudice but of a familiar juvenile compulsion to hear the sound of falling glass.

Unofficially, things have not been so rosy. There are large, modern garden-apartment developments in Mount Vernon where ways are found to circumvent New York's anti-discrimination statutes and in which no Negro can rent a unit. There are still neighborhood property-owners' associations that seek to prevent or rigidly limit Negro encroachment. And there are real estate promoters, some of them Negro, who have attempted to use the block-busting technique—that is, to panic white property owners into taking flight and selling at a loss so that they in turn can sell the property at a high mark-up to Negroes, and in the process create another all-colored neighborhood.

And there are, of course, the subtle personal discriminations—the small affronts, the chilly attitude, the physical turning-away of a next-door neighbor.

Still, most of these middle-class Negro migrants have found Mount Vernon tolerable.

Dunbar S. McLaurin, Ph.D., University of Illinois, practicing attorney, economic consultant, and real estate speculator, takes obvious pride and pleasure in his spacious $50,000-plus home on one of Mount Vernon's finest streets. He is even philosophical about the fact that he probably paid ten per cent extra for it because he is a Negro.

Like any newcomer to suburbia he likes to show off the extensive lawn, talk about plans for the garden, and display the report card that shows how well his little girl has adjusted to her new school, where she is one of only four nonwhites. ("Well-mannered and cooperative," the teacher had written, "a little lady and a fine addition to our group.")

"A couple of years ago Liz and I decided we had to get out of Harlem," McLaurin explains. "We were tired of living in an apartment, and the public schools were so bad we had to put the kid in a private school. Liz figured we could afford to go, and you know how that is—I figured we had to afford to go.

"We looked at some of those places on up the river around New Rochelle, those big old estates with elevators and wine cellars and nine bathrooms and all that. You can get a real bargain up there in a way, and all that grandeur is especially tempting to a Negro. But Liz is a practical woman. She said, 'If the rich white people who owned these places can't keep them up, how can we? We don't have to take a white elephant just because we're Negro.' But a lot of them have, and there are whole colored neighborhoods up there."

The house the McLaurins finally found in Mount Vernon is of the 1920's vintage, solidly built and luxuriously finished with bookcases, fireplaces, built-in cabinets, and the spacious halls and rooms of the period. Elizabeth McLaurin, who grew up in Birmingham and has the soft accent, bubbling laugh, and fluid grace of the Southern belle, has been busy decorating it with restrained taste.

"Oh, Lord, there are all kinds of things wrong with it. But it's big and comfortable and it's such a joy to be out of the city."

Close your eyes and listen to the bright social conversation of the McLaurins and the white and colored neighbors who have dropped by for an evening and you can believe you are listening to any group of young-married and early-middle-aged couples anywhere: children and schools, community agencies and the new traffic regulations on the superhighway, taxes and local politics, flowers and the new spring hats.

Still The Problem comes in—muted and not active and festering as in the ghettos, but nevertheless real, and with some strange twists. It takes on the shape of status here, rather than simply race.

Jewell Cobb, doctor of biology, a cancer researcher at Bellevue Medical Center, and beginning next fall a teacher at Sarah Lawrence College, relates a remarkable tale.

"We moved out about three years ago into a neighborhood not far from here. There were a few Negro families, but not too many, and all our relations were good. We had an interracial neighborhood association and we really worked on our local problems together. Why"—and here she flashes a smile of conscious irony—"some of my best friends are whites.

"But the neighborhood has continued to become more and more Negro. We never had any formal quota arrangement in our old association, but informally we could have arranged to hold down the percentage of Negroes and discourage the undesirables. I'm sure some of the block-busting real estate promoters got into the act, and then some of the whites just kept drifting away for other reasons—wanting to get farther out and into new houses.

"So now we have a new neighborhood association—and this one is all Negro. They're people who have just come out from the city and when my husband came back from their first meeting I asked him what he thought. 'They're bitter and aggressive,' he said, 'and that's all the program they've got. They don't say so, but they want to run out the rest of the whites.'"

This is obviously distressing to Dr. Cobb. She and her

husband, the first Negro hired as a junior executive by
Mutual of New York, found in Mount Vernon that their
race problem had been reduced to such relatively minor
irritations as the inability of their children to join their
white friends for a swim at a private beach club. Now
the newcomers are threatening to rebuild the ghetto
around them.

This tendency is a matter of concern, too, to Mrs. Clar-
ence Pair, a suburban matron who has long been the firm-
handed arbiter of Mount Vernon's Negro society, and
who takes obvious satisfaction in her ability to trace antecedents back to the ancient glories of Charleston, South
Carolina.

"We've always had good relations and stability here in
Mount Vernon. Why, all our charitable and civic boards
are interracial; I've been serving on some of them for
twenty years. It is ridiculous for Negroes to talk about
forming separate groups to try to take over things. What
we need to do is work together the way we always have."

This, of course, is conservative talk, befitting any spacious living room in a Westchester suburb. It carries over
to politics, too. Dr. Pair, who formerly practiced in Harlem but now maintains both his home and office in Westchester, contributes regularly to the Republican party and
worries about the trend toward socialized medicine.

"I don't care what the younger people argue," he says
firmly, "President Eisenhower is doing a good job, and

he is right when he says these things take time. There's too much of a tendency to rush, these days."

It applies even to Dunbar McLaurin, who bears one of the proud names of the Negro protest movement. His father was the schoolteacher who brought the famous McLaurin test case which opened the University of Oklahoma to Negroes, and invalidated the effort to segregate them on the campus.

"Liz and I just don't have time to practice sociology," he says. "We like it out here, we're being treated all right, and the neighbors are either friendly or let us alone. I'm just too busy to worry about anything but my own affairs."

The only really liberal talk comes from a white couple, Mr. and Mrs. Fred Williams. He is a prosperous New York accountant, and she has studied sociology and still practices it. She is convinced that there are no real racial tensions in Mount Vernon, that the interracial patterns in the neighborhoods will endure, and that things will continue to get better and better in every way. She also had no doubt that Hubert Humphrey would be elected president.

Riding in the traditional Volkswagen down to the traditional night-time desertion of the commuter's station, the talk turns in the worn grooves of suburbia. The speaker is Harold Wood, practicing attorney of Mount Vernon, Republican, and the first Negro in history to sit on the Westchester County Board of Supervisors. He talks fondly of the town that has been good to him:

"I worry about the failure of these professional Negroes to become more active in community affairs. They tend to stay sort of withdrawn after they get out here. I'm not talking about politics or special Negro problems. We haven't really got many of those anyway. The local NAACP chapter is pretty much a paper organization; I found that out when I served as president.

"I'm not saying we don't have problems. But we've got less than most, and if we can look at them objectively we'll find that some of them at least are our fault as much as anybody's. How can we expect people to be glad to have us as neighbors unless we pitch in and do our share in civic matters?

"I guess I'm a pretty fair example of what I'm talking about. I started practicing law here ten years ago, and like any kid with a new diploma I had my troubles getting started. I could have gone into a partnership but I decided to try it alone. When you do that you've got to have help from the established lawyers, and I got it—from white lawyers, too, who sent cases my way. I tried to pay it back by working in any way I could to help the community, and of course I got around and saw people all over town. When I decided to go into politics it wasn't any matter of window-dressing and balancing a ticket and that sort of thing. I got votes in every district, and I carried some all-white boxes. That's the way I look at this job, too, to represent everybody in Mount Vernon.

"The way I see it, the white people who are being displaced were the ones who really worked for the community. They put the Community Chest over the top, and they went out and rang the doorbells for the Cancer Fund, and kept the PTA's going. If we are going to replace them we've got to fill that gap. I'm getting some of these folks together on Sunday morning for breakfast down at the hotel to talk this over, and I hope I can fire 'em up and get 'em moving."

Supervisor Woods tilts back his narrow-brimmed hat, plunges his hands into the pockets of his white Ivy League raincoat, gazes around the deserted square, and speaks the eternal words of the booster:

"By golly, this has always been a good town, and we've got to get together and keep it that way."

CHAPTER 9

THE WALLS
OF FEAR

IN THEIR more than four hundred years of residence
on this continent, from the slave quarters of the Old
South to the ghettos of today's great industrial cities,
Negroes for the most part have lived apart from whites.

In the South they were walled off by the legal barriers
now being systematically struck down by the United
States Supreme Court. Elsewhere their comparatively recent arrival in force has produced extra-legal devices for
residential segregation which, although often contrary to
declared public policy, have effectively reproduced the
Southern pattern of all-colored neighborhoods.

The shoulders of whites and Negroes rub increasingly
in the workplace, in public institutions, in the market-
place, and in areas of public accommodation. But when
the whistle blows, or the wall clock marks the end of the

work day, the paths of homing whites and Negroes sharply diverge.

In the rush hour a northbound New York subway starts out with a richly mixed human cargo. On the journey uptown the whites steadily thin out until, as the train pounds across the shifting boundary of Harlem, only Negroes and Puerto Ricans are left.

For some, and perhaps for most Negroes, a segregated neighborhood provides a welcome retreat from a white world that can be hostile when it is not indifferent. Dirty, crowded, generally depressed the home territory may be, but it still represents a haven where a black man can relax with his own kind, immune to great indignities and small affronts.

For others—and their number increases with the rapid growth of the new Negro middle class—the rigid, invisible walls are a source of mounting frustration.

For the community at large the Negro ghetto stands as a great unresolved social problem, a focus of poverty, vice, crime, and human misery that can spread its infections through the whole of the body politic.

For reasonably well-to-do Negroes as well as the very poor, housing ranks as the number one problem—the greatest single source of privation and of grievance. A Negro still encounters prejudice and discrimination in every area of everyday living. However, in employment, education, politics, and free access to public institutions and services, an optimistic colored man can now see daylight. Despite a great deal of talk, and some action, the slum in which he lives remains uncleared; nowhere has progress kept pace with the spread of urban blight.

The 1950 census provided these measurements:

More than 60 per cent of all urban Negro families lived in substandard dwellings—units either dilapidated or lacking minimum sanitary facilities. The percentage of whites in such dwellings was less than 20 per cent.

More than a third of urban dwellings occupied by Negroes were classified as crowded by a rather primitive standard; that is, containing more persons than rooms. Only one white family in eight lived under similar conditions.

There is no reason to believe that the data collected by the census-takers in 1960 will substantially alter this dismal picture.

These are only the rough dimensions of the Negro housing problem. The dwellings available to colored tenants or purchasers are usually in jam-packed areas deficient in parks, playgrounds, and public services, and served by the oldest and most decrepit of public schools. In many cases the neighborhoods are threaded among industrial and commercial districts. The Negro often finds himself lodged uncertainly in housing that is slated to make way for nonresidential structures and therefore is subject to no more maintenance and upkeep than casually enforced laws may require of his landlord.

With all of this, square foot for square foot, and in terms of services rendered, the Negro usually pays more for housing than any other class of our citizens. Great profits in slum property are still possible for a callous investor; that such are still around is indicated by the tales of calculated exploitation that fill the docket of New York City's special housing court.

There has been a sporadic public assault on the urban slums over more than two decades, and tangible results can be seen in every city. Harlem provides a notable example, with great areas of mouldering tenements sawed away to make room for low-rent public housing and so-called Title One medium-income private housing. The process is so well-advanced that the district, river-bound in its upper reaches, may actually show a decline in population as a result of wholesale reductions in population density.

The trouble is that the tide of Negro and Puerto Rican newcomers still runs ahead of the bulldozers of slum clearance. The patchwork program, operating in fits and starts in response to recurring economy waves in Washington and onslaughts from private real estate lobbyists, cleans up a corner of one slum but may send a surplus of displaced residents out to found another depressed neighborhood somewhere else.

Even so, the results produced by low-rent public hous-

ing in the lower reaches of the Negro housing problem
are impressive. Negro families enabled by public sub-
sidy to move into these projects make an astronomical improvement in their physical environment, and the process
is producing measurable results in the rising generation.
It seems reasonable to assume that public housing as a
basic tool of urban renewal is now firmly built into federal policy, and that the coming change in the political cli-
mate in Washington will bring a new priority and vigor to
the program.

Although all public housing is now theoretically un-
segregated, and a considerable amount in fringe neighborhoods is so in fact, it still follows that the program will
tend to perpetuate segregated neighborhoods. Even when
cleared slum land is put to nonresidential use and the
former residents of the area are physically relocated some
distance away, the separate pattern is likely to re-emerge.
Indeed, the evidence is quite clear that Negroes of the
lower income and attainment level will huddle together
by choice, even without the strictures of prejudice. Lester
Granger of the Urban League conceded this when he said:
"So long as we have this continuing flood of migrants in
New York, we would need Harlem and other substantially segregated neighborhoods as receiving depots if for
no other reason. People want to, and probably need to,
stay among their own kind when they are strangers trying

to make a new life in unfamiliar surroundings."

No one, then, has reason to assume that the segregated Negro sections of the great cities will disappear any time soon—although in every one of them internal improvement of environment and services is a matter of urgent public business.

The great, unresolved problem is to make provision for the increasing number of Negro families who have climbed the ladder to the middle class. Like their white counterparts, who emerged from the same ghettos a generation or more before them, they want to remove themselves and their children from the slums, and they have income sufficient to pay their own way. Except for a hardy few in the higher income brackets, however, they are simply denied the right to resettle as they see fit.

Other ethnic and religious minorities have encountered the same barriers in the past—and for some, notably Jews, restrictions still exist. But no other American suffers restraints on his mobility comparable to those reserved for nonwhites. The attorney general of Michigan has publicized an elaborate scale employed by real estate operators and property-owners in the select suburbs of Grosse Point to determine acceptability of prospective home purchasers. The computations were based on such matters as accent, swarthiness, dress, manner, educational attainment, and the like, and the minimum passing grade was 50 out of a possible 100 points. There was no provision for Negroes at all.

There are, of course, reasons aside from simple race prejudice why barriers go up against a Negro who wants to buy a house or rent an apartment in an area occupied by whites. There is a widespread fear among property-owners and real estate men that the advent of a single Negro family brings on an inundation. This is clearly without foundation in upper-income areas, where the scarcity of prosperous Negro families is a guarantee against any sharply rising black tide. And the Commission on Race and Housing has found in extensive nationwide surveys that this does not necessarily follow even in moderate-income communities. Where whites have accepted a few Negro families as part of the normal turnover they have found no substantial change in the character of the neighborhood, and they have often found the Negro newcomers as anxious as they to keep the area from going all-black.

A Negro doctor who was one of the first arrivals in a white neighborhood in Baltimore went from house to house urging his neighbors not to take flight, and wryly warning them of the result. "I'm moving out here because I don't want to raise my children in a Negro slum. If you move away and this becomes a Negro slum, don't think you can get away from me—because I'll be moving right behind you."

Across the country there has now been enough experience with mixed neighborhoods to put to practical test the theory that the entry of nonwhites automatically undercuts property values—a theory, the Commission on Race and Housing has found, held and acted upon by many real estate brokers, mortgage lenders and property appraisers "almost as an article of faith." The Commission's surveys show that the effect on property values of such a transition is determined by a variety of factors. The range of possibilities is set forth in the Commission's summary report, *Where Shall We Live?*:

> More often than not, residential areas which nonwhites are permitted to enter are older neighborhoods where the housing is already obsolescent or deteriorating. Declining values in those districts, coinciding with nonwhite entry, have furnished much of the "evidence" for the thesis that nonwhites injure property values. In reality, values in those areas would decline in any case; the demand of incoming nonwhites for housing, replacing the loss of white demand, probably tends more often to support rather than depress the housing market in older neighborhoods.
>
> Much depends on the reaction of white residents to the coming of minorities. If the whites hasten to leave, the market may be glutted by an oversupply

of houses offered for sale in a short period. Then, the expectation of a fall in property values becomes a "self-fulfilling prophecy." Whites predict that values will drop with the entry of nonwhites, and when the entry occurs, they act in a manner to make the prediction realized.

On the other hand, if white residents of an area are in no hurry to leave, but nonwhites are eager to come in, the pressure of nonwhite demand may bid up the price of houses. Several situations of this type have been observed, with market values of property rising during a period of racial transition.

In a third type of situation, whites may not rush to leave an area but nonwhite demand may be weak, and the presence of nonwhites may discourage demand from whites. In these circumstances a decline of house prices is probable. In some cases which have been studied, however, the presence of a limited number of nonwhites in a good residential district or housing development seems not to have discouraged seriously white interest in the area. Interracial neighborhoods have come into existence, with both whites and nonwhites active as both buyers and sellers, and values have remained stable.

In general, the conclusion seems warranted that nonwhite entry into residential areas does not necessarily depress real estate market values. Under certain conditions it may increase values. Among neighborhoods actually investigated for this Commission, in cities on both coasts and in midcontinent, the entry of nonwhites was found to have had either no effect or a favorable effect on property-selling prices in the majority of cases.

These, however, are only facts, and as the Commission concedes, they are often less important as a motive for action than what the people affected believe to be facts. The sensitive area of housing produces an array of rationalizations by whites to politely cloak the unreasoning fear that provides their real motive for resistance—that any but the most formal contact with Negroes will somehow lead to a collapse of social standards and ultimately to wholesale miscegenation.

A man does not depart from respectability when he insists that his opposition to a Negro newcomer in the neighborhood is based solely on his proper, conservative concern for maintaining property values; he may even say, and believe, that he personally has no objection to associating with colored people and that he is acting only in the interest of the community. But when the pressure is really on, as it has been in the Chicago suburb of Deerfield, the veneer is likely to be stripped away in a fashion that Northerners find peculiarly painful. There, as the community split sharply over the advent of an integrated

private housing project, many a middle-class family of
Abolitionist antecedents took its stand openly for white
supremacy. At an open meeting one native of the Abe
Lincoln country stated the case as bluntly as it can be
put: "We moved out here in the first place to get away
from the Jews, and we'll be damned if we'll stand still
while the niggers move in."

Here, too, the facts seem to indicate that such adamant
prejudice is held by only a relatively small minority of the
white population, a number probably about equal to those
at the other end of the spectrum who are committed to
integration as a matter of moral principle. The best guess
is that the views of something like 75 per cent of the urban
population of the North and West range between these
two poles, without any really strong feeling either way.
Moreover, the trend is toward greater tolerance.

In 1942 the National Opinion Research Center put this
question to a national cross-section of whites: "If a Negro
family with the same income and education moved into
your block would it make any difference to you?" Among
non-Southerners, 42 per cent of the respondents said it
would make no difference, with 12 per cent in the South
giving the same reply. Fourteen years later, in 1956, the
proportion in the North stating no objection had risen to
58 per cent, with a remarkable 38 per cent recorded in
the South.

It must be noted, however, that these were replies to an

abstract question, and it is a measure of the ambivalence of the white American attitude on race that in many cases the answers would probably have been reversed had the query been: "A Negro family is moving in next door to you tomorrow. Do you mind?" Gunnar Myrdal long ago defined the Negro problem in America as a conflict between equalitarian ideals and discriminatory practice.

In many instances the naked race prejudice of the few is translated into action by the majority in terms of status. This is demonstrated by the fact that the most determined resistance to Negro entry is often to be found in those neighborhoods which a generation or less ago were staked out by members of religious and ethnic minorities who were themselves rising above the ghetto. A broad thoroughfare in the Bronx rimmed with the neat cliff-dwellings of middle-class Jewish families is referred to by Negroes as "The Great White Way." Cruising through the neighborhood, an officer of the Bronx chapter of the NAACP says, "It's easy for me to get a contribution here—but it is impossible to get an apartment."

Even those old-line whites whose secure social position gives them less concern with the symbols of status are likely to find their tolerance smothered by pressures for conformity. The issue of race is, as it has always been, controversial, no matter which side a man takes; the white who embraces it in any fashion will find himself under sharp emotional attack that will brand him, at the mildest, as eccentric. In the gray flannel set this can have practical consequences. Ed Crilly, a young advertising executive and Republican leader of Deerfield, has noted the result when the racial controversy there erupted in the metropolitan newspapers: "Many of the fellows in Deerfield were told by their bosses in Chicago to ignore this whole issue, and that is just what they have done—kept from getting involved." *The New York Times Magazine* has reported that one who didn't, Charles Rippey, found it necessary to terminate his association with a leading Chicago law firm after he joined the board of the interracial housing corporation.

It is worthy of note that the resistance to neighborhood integration appears to be considerably less among the younger householders than among their elders. This may reflect improving educational standards and a general broadening of the social consciousness, as well as the fact that conservatism generally keeps pace with the hardening of the arteries. But it undoubtedly also has to do with the practical experience of the members of the younger generation, who have accepted an essential rootlessness as a way of life. In urbia, suburbia, and exurbia the neighborhood no longer exists in the sentimental terms we still tend to apply to it. Today it is rare indeed to find a man raising his children in the house his father built, and expecting the generations to march on under the old roof after he has gone. It is unusual, even, to find a young married couple expecting to finish out their own days in the dwelling they presently occupy. Mobility has long since eroded the social unity of the American neighborhood; it is today made up of families who have no more contact with their neighbors than they choose to have.

However, the racial barriers still stand, despite federal court rulings and a variety of state and local laws aimed against them. So long as they do, there can be only one answer to the pertinent question directed to the American conscience by Earl B. Schwulst, president and chairman of the board of New York's Bowery Savings Bank, and chairman of the Commission on Race and Housing:

"Can a man be said to be truly free when, because of his color, he cannot buy or rent a home in the neighborhood of his choice?"

CHAPTER 10

THE USES
OF LAW

F OR MORE than two decades the great national battle-ground for Negro rights has been in the courts.

The victories have been famous, culminating in the final reversal of the old *Plessy v. Ferguson* separate-but-equal doctrine and the establishment of a precedent by the United States Supreme Court that effectively bans any form of official discrimination against Negroes.

The grand strategy was designed by the National Association for the Advancement of Colored People, and NAACP lawyers led by Thurgood Marshall argued the case at the bar. This in itself was a matter of considerable significance; in the crusade to remove the legal buttresses of second-class citizenship Negroes for the first time provided their own leadership, and the white liberals who supported their cause faded into the rear ranks.

The actual orders issued in the historic series of court cases were directed at the Southern states, which had translated the custom of racial segregation into law. But the impact was felt by colored people everywhere, from Harlem to Bandung.

A Negro psychologist, Kenneth Clark of New York University, believes the climactic Brown decision of 1954, which outlawed segregation in the public schools, marked an emotional turning-point for American Negroes as significant as that occasioned by the Emancipation Proclamation.

"Consciously or unconsciously, and no matter how much we might rebel against it, we all had accepted the fact of second-class status," he says. "The Jim Crow cases that came before, important as they were, didn't directly approach the basic point. The Brown decision did—and for the first time every Negro *felt* that he was a man in his own right and that his government would help him prove it."

This, in Clark's view, in the end will prove far more important than the slow and painful process of school desegregation that has been initiated in the South. In his own case, it was in part at least the psychological impact of the Brown decision that prompted him to assume a key role in the extra-legal battle to minimize the *de facto* segregation that still exists in New York's public schools.

Although spokesmen from the New York Urban League

and other organizations originally pleaded before the New York City Board of Education for the program that its numerous critics have called forced integration of the city's schools, it was Clark who called the shots. He accepted as a premise the fact that the segregated neighborhoods which produced segregated schools in New York could not be abolished overnight. But the segregation which produced inferior schools and subjected the children who attended them to special handicaps, he insisted, could be ended by direct action. He proposed, in essence, that children be shuffled about in the system without regard to residence or attendance area so that genuine integration would be universal.

"The Supreme Court had said that segregation in the schools inhibited the students who were subjected to it, and I agreed," Clark says. "I thought that was just as true in New York as it was in Little Rock."

Residential segregation still produces school segregation in New York, as it does in every major American city, but Clark contends that the two-year campaign has produced significant results. The latest report of the New York City Board of Education shows a decline in segregated elementary schools from 62.6 per cent in 1957 to 56.7 per cent in 1959—a segregated school being one with 90 per cent enrollment from one race. There have been changes in administrative personnel, and in policy, which are at least based on the principle Clark espoused, and he believes that important precedents have been set that will in time apply in all the non-Southern public school systems.

The Negro struggle for equality in education has been the focus of national attention in recent years, and was, of course, the initial cause of the Southern resistance that has made headlines around the world. But outside the South, Negroes have been pressing on many other fronts, with notable legal and practical results.

Most lawyers, and very probably most members of the United States Supreme Court, feel that precedent-making by interpretation of the Constitution—or, as in the Brown case, re-interpretation—has gone about as far as it can go. The public policy is now sharply and unmistakably defined: there can be no discrimination on the basis of race in any public activity; that is, any activity conducted under public authority or supported by public funds. The rulings in the area of private activity are more shadowy, but an impressive number of state and local statutes have been enacted and so far have withstood the test of litigation.

Here, however, the further extension of law is likely to involve a fundamental and perhaps irreconcilable conflict of principle—between regulation in the name of common justice on the one hand, and the individual's right of privacy on the other. The usual tests of the public character of an institution are about exhausted: direct financial support by government as in schools, colleges, and housing projects; indirect financial support as in the case of government-guaranteed housing loans; public regulation as in the case of common carriers; licensing as in the case of bars and restaurants; the common law concept of the obligations of the innkeeper to serve the whole public. But the Negro drive for equal treatment in every area is no longer limited by narrow concepts of legality.

This was dramatically illustrated by the Negro college students' sit-in campaign in the South, and its support by white and Negro pickets across the country. Had the Negro students consulted the more cautious lawyers of the NAACP in advance, they doubtless would have been advised that they were in serious danger of violating the law. They could parade on the public sidewalk with their signs of protest and remain within the protection of the constitutional guarantee of free speech; when they went inside a variety store lunch room to take a stand on private property and refused to obey an order to leave they were quite clearly guilty of trespassing, as the courts have subsequently held. The college students, of course, were not interested in legal niceties but in results, and were quite prepared to take the Negro protest movement beyond the orderly procedures of the law and the prospect of final, binding settlement in court.

In the same vein Ralph Bunche, who operates these days under the diplomatic restraints of his high position with

THE USES OF LAW · 125

the United Nations and is not much given to personal protest on racial matters, felt constrained to make public complaint when the Forest Hills Tennis Club barred his son. The challenge was made on moral rather than legal grounds, but it was nevertheless aimed at the right of a private and essentially social organization to use race as a basis for determining its membership. While such discrimination may well be a legitimate extension of the members' right of privacy, it stands as no less a personal affront to the minority group against whom it is invoked. Not many of these are capable of assuming the philosophical attitude of David Cohn, who once wrote that he considered such matters irrelevant because he didn't care to associate with the kind of people who belong to clubs that bar Jews.

Anti-discrimination laws, while they vary widely in intent, effectiveness, and in the stringency of their enforcement, are now on the books of most non-Southern states. They are aimed, for the most part, at the bread-and-butter level of daily living. In underlying principle they reduce to irrelevancy the Congressional civil-rights measures which serve as political symbols and regularly produce Southern filibusters, deadlock Congress, and sunder the Democratic Party.

New York, where anti-discrimination laws go back to 1881, has long been the leader in the field. The state's fair employment act, passed in 1945, was the first in the nation. In 1952 the law was amended to cover discrimination in places of public accommodation, and in 1955–1956 was extended to publicly assisted housing.

In an official pamphlet published in 1959 Governor Nelson Rockefeller proudly proclaimed: "The state's laws on discrimination are unsurpassed in the United States." Whether the claim still stands up may now be open to question. In the closing days of the 1960 Assembly session in Albany, a bill to outlaw discrimination in private housing was choked to death in a legislative bottleneck, and the Democrats laid the blame on the governor's doorstep. In this regard New York now lags behind Massachusetts, Connecticut, Washington, Colorado, and Oregon—although New York City is enforcing a local ordinance carrying similar provisions.

A legal declaration against discrimination, and an end to it in practice, are two very different things. In New York the enormous task of implementing the statutes is charged to the State Commission Against Discrimination. In its fourteen years of operation, SCAD has pioneered many of the techniques now employed by similar agencies in other states.

SCAD's chairman and chief executive officer is Elmer Carter, a massive, very dark man who came to the agency at its inception from a background of social work with the Urban League.

"The primary requirements for this kind of undertaking are patience and common sense," Carter says. "The laws have teeth, of course. We can issue orders, and obtain the sanction of the courts if they are not obeyed. But the main tools are conference and conciliation. You've not only got to get a man into a job or a housing unit or a hotel, you've got to get him accepted."

Any person may file a discrimination complaint with SCAD in any of its three areas of jurisdiction—employment, public accommodation, or public housing. One of the five commissioners is then assigned to investigate. He may dismiss the complaint or, finding probable cause, begin the process of consultation and conciliation with the offending employer, labor union, public official, or proprietor. If that fails, there is a public hearing culminating in dismissal or in an order to cease and desist.

The Commission also has the power, which Carter considers of first importance, to initiate an investigation without a specific complaint if there is reason to suspect discriminatory practices. This may be directed against an individual employer or proprietor, or it may take the form of a class action—as it did in late 1959 when SCAD decided to move not on the suspicion but on the certainty that Negroes could not find accommodations in many of New York's upstate resort areas.

In this instance roving teams of Commissioners and staff members didn't waste time investigating, but simply went into the little mountain and lake towns and called meetings of public officials and local bonifaces. There the discussions proceeded on the undisputed assumption that Negroes would not be accommodated, and the SCAD representatives patiently listened to the proprietors explain why this was so.

"This is not a matter of making accusations, bringing charges, or even of preaching the gospel," Carter says. "In most cases these people are simply scared, and it is understandable that they should be. They're small operators for the most part—a couple, usually, who've got every cent they own tied up in a motel or a restaurant, and a mortgage besides. They work like the devil trying to attract people to come to their places, and they're afraid that if they let one Negro in the word will get around and the whites will stay away. Most of them will say they are sorry that's the way it is, and a lot of them mean it.

"We can't honestly ignore such fears, or simply dismiss them out of hand. We try to ease them as much as we can by pointing out the generally good experience we have had elsewhere. And the most effective thing we do is point out that if everybody in town adopts an open policy and sticks to it, nobody can really be hurt. We usually begin to make progress when we can convince the group that we are just as practical as they are."

The case load was slightly off, but 1959 was a typical year for SCAD. Of the 794 complaints, 84.5 per cent pertained to employment, 10.1 per cent to places of public accommodation, and 5.4 per cent to public housing. Color was the alleged basis of discrimination in 67.5 per cent of these cases; creed (primarily Jewish), place of national origin (primarily Puerto Rican), and age accounted for the rest.

It is human nature to fancy personal grievances where none exist—or at least are not subject to verification. SCAD rejects a surprisingly high total of the complaints received. In 1959 a total of 1,187 cases, including some carried over from the year before, were officially closed; probable cause to sustain charges of discrimination was found in only 199. Consultation and conciliation settled all but ten.

This may seem like a lot of work for so little direct, tangible result. But Carter insists that the very existence of the laws, and of the agency to enforce them, has produced marked changes in New York.

"Particularly in the beginning," he said, "there were many cases in which employers were personally willing to hire Negroes, but were afraid to because they thought their other employees or their customers would object. Once the law was on the books they could go ahead, and if anybody protested they could point to the statute and say they didn't have any choice.

"It worked that way in hotels, bars, and restaurants, too, when the law was broadened in 1952. I think there were many proprietors who were actually relieved to have someone else resolve an issue that had been bothering them for a long time. They had a good excuse to serve Negroes—and as it turned out, only in rare cases did anyone really object."

Carter would be the last to claim that all discrimination has ended in New York.

"There are thousands of cases we never hear about, and there are hundreds of ways of getting around us even when we do. You can technically obey the law, and in subtle ways simply make it so unpleasant for a colored person that he can't stay around. But we have managed to open up whole new areas of employment for Negroes and, as always, experience is the best teacher. Employers find out that Negroes can be good workers and pleasant people to have around—and another door has been opened, and the word is spread."

On his gloomier days, Carter cheers himself by gazing down upon the streets of the financial district which spread away from SCAD's headquarters in a tall building on Lower Broadway.

"When we first set up shop fourteen years ago, you could look down there at the lunch hour and you wouldn't see a single colored girl unless she happened to be a charwoman. Now, when they come pouring out of the offices Negroes are dotted among the secretaries and clerical workers. I remember how the first few used to carry themselves—rigid and uncertain, as though they were walking on eggs. Now they swing along just like the rest, and you can see their confidence.

"Of course SCAD isn't solely responsible for the change. All manner of forces have been at work, including a general softening of white attitudes. And education among Negroes, training them for better jobs and making them want them. But maybe it was SCAD that first held out the hope that decent employment would be waiting if they stuck to their schooling instead of giving up and taking a menial job. Anyway, I like to look down there and see those girls walking along in the sun. It's my personal vision of progress."

CHAPTER 11

THE CHANGING
GUARD

A NEGRO journalist, Louis E. Lomax, has written for *Harper's* an epitaph for the National Association for the Advancement of Colored People, and appended a sort of marble footnote to record the prior demise of the Urban League.

The lunch counter sit-in demonstrations of Southern Negro college students, Lomax writes, "were proof that the Negro leadership class, epitomized by the NAACP, was no longer the prime mover of the Negro's social revolt."

"This revolt," Lomax continues, "swelling underground for the past two decades, means the end of the traditional Negro leadership class. Local organization leaders were caught flat-footed by the demonstrations; the parade had moved off without them. In a series of almost frantic moves this spring, they lunged to the front and shouted loud, but they were scarcely more than a cheering section —leaders no more."

Lomax' reliability as a witness in these matters inevitably has been challenged, and his case is weakened by his conscious stance as an aging Angry Young Man. Even so, he has reduced to the type of an eminently respectable national magazine a complaint that can be heard in every Negro community from Boston to Los Angeles.

In part this is an emotional reaction to the quickening drumbeat of African revolt, and to the spectacular forays of the Southern college students who have broken out of the orderly channels of legal protest against discrimination.

In part it is a symbolic picking-up of the gauntlet thrown down by the white extremists of the South, who have preached economic boycott, threatened terror, and lit the fuse of an occasional stick of dynamite.

Thurgood Marshall, the NAACP counsel, who probably retains more favor among the disaffected than any of his contemporaries, rang no bells when he proclaimed in a speech reviewing "The Fifty Year Fight for Civil Rights": "We are still determined that regardless of what tactics are used against us, we will not get down in the gutter with the people seeking to serve any unconstitutional mode of government."

There is a direct echo of Booker T. Washington here, and the answer, enunciated in the inordinately precise accents of the young Negro intellectual, might well be: Why not?

The embattled Negro leaders can offer reasons based on practical considerations as well as principle. They can point to a record of steadily accelerating gains on almost every front, and demonstrate from the record that these were made possible by a working coalition between Negroes and white liberals. They can argue in terms of tactics and logistics, pointing out that in every significant sector Negroes are a minority without sufficient weight to press their own cause unaided, and citing the undeniable fact that every important organized effort in the past has been largely financed by white sympathizers.

The rebuttal comes more from the heart than the head. Lomax states it in these terms: "The Negro masses will name leaders and give them power and responsibility. But there will never again be another class of white-oriented leaders such as the one that has prevailed since 1900."

For better or for worse, Lomax may very well be right.

But if the break with the old leadership has come, or is on the way, the replacements for the present distinguished company of tacticians, persuaders, advocates, and conciliators are not yet in sight.

So far, when the Negro masses have turned away from the established group to name their own leaders and confer upon them power and responsibility they most often have come up with Adam Clayton Powell or someone of like character and less innate ability. Over the years Powell has discharged his responsibility largely by breaking his pursuit of personal pleasure with periods of intense and sometimes pointless agitation.

In his eight terms in Congress, Powell has initiated, or been instrumental in passing, few measures of practical value to the Negro people. At the same time he has sabotaged a number of housing, education and other social measures of prime benefit through his adamant insistence on appending sometimes practically meaningless anti-discrimination clauses. He concedes his maverick role, and defends it:

"I'm an irritant. That's it, and I see myself that way. Just keep on turning the screw, turning the screw. Drip, drip, drip makes a hole in the marble."

Speaking before Princeton University's Cliosophic Society, Powell turned his fire directly on the present Negro leadership even while borrowing a thesis and a good deal of language from one of its distinguished members, Professor John Hope Franklin of Brooklyn College. "The last revolutionary is the Negro," Powell proclaimed, taking the line directly from an eloquent article written by Franklin for the Urban League.

Franklin had put the case this way:

Not only does his Americanism compel the Negro to strive to improve his own status by demanding the rights that are his. It also gives him, as it gives to others committed to the ideals set forth in the American dream, a burning desire to make the system work. He is the acid test of the system, and he knows it. . . . He is a proud American who wants to make Americanism work.

Powell somehow took off from this point and wound up with this:

The thrust of the Negro mass has impaled accidentally the Northern "liberal." The thrust of the Negro today is sweeping away from underneath him the foundations upon which he has stood so long—that of being the Great White Father or the Great White Mother of the Negro people. Desperately, with contrived organizations and committees plus certain captive Negroes—and that is a refined phrase for Uncle Tom—the Northern "liberal" is trying to hold on.

This is not a new line with the preacher-politician. He was, as he has done over a period of several years, returning prior fire directed at him by spokesmen for the NAACP and other Negro leaders who have publicly branded him a "racist demagogue." The term plainly stings Powell, but it has not deterred him in his sustained effort to play upon the emotions of the Negro people—as, indeed, it practically could not since this is the single technique that holds together his solid political following despite his well-publicized personal and political peccadilloes.

Powell is an adequate symbol of the difficulties that increasingly beset responsible Negro leaders—and, although in the nature of the human condition they do not recognize it, the mass of Negro people themselves. There is a genuine cause, and in the terms of the everyday lives of Negroes it is a pressing one. The members of an embattled minority do not take to the long, philosophical view; they respond to crude symbols, and their reaction is likely to be glandular.

Under these circumstances, complicated as they are by the generally lower educational level of the Negro people, it is no more possible to conduct a rational debate on the race issue within the Negro community than it is within the impassioned and disturbed white community of the South.

The Negro leader who tries immediately finds himself assailed on the ground that he has joined the white enemy camp to shore up his own status in the larger community —and it is further argued that in the rarefied atmosphere of the national interracial movements he has lost touch with the Negro masses. In an earlier time, when Negro ministers and educators spoke for the colored community in seeking concessions from the dominant whites, the term of opprobrium was "Uncle Tom," an invocation of the stereotype of the servile Negro currying favor by tugging his forelock in the presence of his masters. Today it is "phony liberal"—and it applies not only to Negroes who deal with whites in high places, but also to the whites with whom they deal.

These two shock words constituted the two-inch-high banner headline under which Harlem's *Amsterdam News* recently reported an offhand remark by former President Truman to the effect that if he were still running a haberdashery he would throw out any customer who trespassed to protest discrimination. Wiped out at a stroke was the long record of Mr. Truman's soul-searing battle for civil rights legislation, in which he held firm even while his party split apart and the Southern wing threatened his re-election.

This sort of thing is the stock in trade of the Negro press, which with only minor exceptions is always sensational, frequently irresponsible, and sometimes venal. Feeding their readers a steady diet of alleged white atrocities and affronts against Negroes, these journals unsheath their long knives against any colored leader who seems to compromise in any degree on a racial issue, and the attack is always personal. In 1957, when the Big Three of national Negro leadership—Roy Wilkins, Martin Luther King, and A. Philip Randolph—reluctantly endorsed a thoroughly watered-down federal civil rights bill as at least better than nothing, the Negro press reacted as though they had sold Adam Clayton Powell down the river.

Louis E. Martin of the *Chicago Defender* acidly inquired: "How silly can you get?" Louis Lautier of the *Afro-American* charged: "Ike charmed the Negro leaders and none of them uttered a word of criticism."

The clamor of the Negro press not only incites but reflects the highly emotional attitude of the Negro community, which makes internal reform extraordinarily difficult and often impossible. One of the abler and more conscientious Negro newspapermen has put it this way: "You charge a race man with wrongdoing that has nothing whatever to do with race, and he charges you with breaking the solid front against the whites and harming the cause. Hit him a second lick, and he'll call you an Uncle Tom and say you've sold out—and it usually works with most of his followers."

In the United States there traditionally has been a great void between the intellectual and the politician. While there were bookish men of philosophical bent among the founders of the republic, and their kind have been called upon in such later seasons of stress as that which produced the New Deal, the day-to-day management of public affairs is usually left to those conditioned in the art of the possible.

In the case of the American Negro, however, the peculiar conditions of his history initially thrust the burden of leadership upon a handful of colored men who pursued their vocation in scholarship or the professions. In response to the Abolitionist tradition, great institutions of higher learning like Oberlin and Harvard admitted favored members of the minority race when almost all other doors to advancement were barred to them. The first Negro leader to receive national recognition was an educator, Booker T. Washington. The man who turned the Negro movement away from Washington's conciliatory policies and endowed it with a new militance was the learned, eloquent, and contentious Brown Brahmin, W.E.B. Du Bois. Although he later displayed marked skill as a negotiator and political fixer, Walter White first won fame as a writer of considerable talent. With the possible exception of A. Phillip Randolph, the tradition carries over to the contemporary Negro spokesmen whose names are most familiar to the general public—Roy Wilkins, Thurgood Marshall, and Henry Lee Moon of the NAACP; Ralph Bunche of the United Nations; Lester Granger of the Urban League; and Martin Luther King, the ministerial disciple of Ghandi who stands as the only leader of consequence yet cast up by the ferment in the South.

It might be argued that these men were the product of a process of natural selection. In the first half of the century the cause required advocates—men who could effectively present the Negro's grievances before the white community. There was more to this than simply pleading for justice. They also had to demonstrate through their eloquence, erudition, and personal conduct the fallacy of the widely held myth of inherent Negro inferiority. Their success, and it has been considerable, was a necessary prerequisite to the more broadly based movement that now threatens to displace them.

They now face the familiar question as to whether the intellectual temperament lends itself to the pedestrian affairs of what increasingly will be an essentially political crusade, depending as it must upon techniques of cajolery and compromise. Certainly the present Negro leaders show the intellectual's usual scorn for practical politicians, the Negro bosses of the colored precincts and their white counterparts as well. Few would take exception to the contemptuous indictment of Edward Holmgren of the Chicago Urban League: "Negro politicians get their patronage and influence in the ward and keep quiet about civil rights, housing, and employment, and do not press for integration." There is justice in the charge. But there is also justice in the counter-complaint of the Negro politicians that the civil-rights issue is an abstraction that doesn't always have direct bearing on the immediate and pressing needs of those who suffer in the swarming ghettos.

In the old days the leadership could operate with a

degree of independence of the Negro people, serving what it deemed to be their best interests without yielding to their whims. This is no longer the case, and no Negro leader has yet appeared who gives promise of surmounting the inevitable personal jealousies that come with prominence, and rallying the diverse forces to common cause.

It is probably true, as many thoughtful Negroes believe, that this condition is transient—a reflection of the dislocations that mark the end of an era. In emotionally rejecting white paternalism, the rising generation of educated Negroes of necessity also rejects the tradition of those leaders who employed it in the time when it was, in fact, essential to Negro progress.

"I guess it's a matter of coming of age," says a reflective old social worker, who himself bears heavy scars inflicted by his own people. "There comes a time when you have to move out on your own. You don't know as much as your elders, but you are past advice and counsel—you have to find out for yourself.

"That's the way it is with those kids on the college campuses down South, and the ones all over the country who are out picketing to support them. Sooner or later, they are going to provide the new Negro leadership anyway. Maybe it's just as well if it's sooner."

CHAPTER 12

THE UNCERTAIN
FUTURE

THE HISTORY of the American Negro is a series of paradoxes, and it may be that another of considerable significance is in the making.

There is more militant talk among Negroes of all classes than the country has ever known, and more concerted pressure against the surviving barriers of segregation, North and South.

At the same time the social ferment seems to be producing a new and impressive cohesion in the Negro community, which heretofore has been held together largely by shared misery. This does not change the objective Negroes long ago set for themselves, but it may change the means by which they will pursue it in the second half of the century.

The goal, of course, remains total acceptance without

discrimination and without prejudice—the ideal that has come to be called integration and, by implication at least, has alarmed many race-proud whites.

Negroes have now begun to acquire a new pride of their own. It is a compound product.

One major element is the vast improvement in the physical circumstances of Negro life. The slums have survived three decades of social reform, and two decades of prosperity, but year by year they have entrapped a diminishing proportion of the Negro people. Thus a steadily increasing number seize the expanding opportunity to shake off the debilitations of inferior environment. In educational attainment and income level these now belong to the middle class, and their drive is to secure the appropriate marks of that status. This is a measure of progress, but it is also a primary source of increased racial tension.

Another element is the psychological impact of the sweeping redefinition of Negro rights by the United States Supreme Court. The outlawing of the legal forms of second-class citizenship in the Southern states has little practical application in other regions of the country, where the barriers are largely extra-legal. But Negroes everywhere have emotionally identified themselves with the symbolic Little Rock Nine; the fortitude of these children has become an epic for a race whose prior heroes were athletes and entertainers who owed their fame to white indulgence.

Finally, the dramatic emergence of free black nations in Africa has given the American Negro the sense of ethnic identification he had always denied himself. Certainly the African heritage, diluted by the passage of centuries and a heavy infusion of white blood, is remote —but now the Negro can look upon it with pride instead of shame.

A light-skinned Negro physician, who had long since attained his own comforts and had never concerned himself personally with racial affairs, discussed the phenomenon with something akin to wonder.

"When I was growing up I never thought about Africa if I could help it," he said. "To me it was a scene in a Tarzan movie, apes swinging through the trees and cannibals and all that. I guess I didn't want to be identified with it, and resented the fact that I was.

"Now when the news comes in from Africa it gives me an emotional wallop. I've never seen those Bantus and I probably never will—and the Lord knows I've got more kinfolks among the whites in America than I have in the Union of South Africa. But somehow it seems like my fight now."

Racial pride can produce undue aggression—as it sometimes does among Negroes these days and doubtless will continue to do in the future. But it can also produce the sense of identity and personal security that was denied

Negroes when they were consigned to a secondary place in a segregated society and subjected without effective recourse to any indignity a white man cared to accord them.

This new pride is the element the curbstone psychologist finds most striking as he examines the shifting racial scene in the great non-Southern cities. It accounts for a certain ambivalence in the attitude of those now inveighing against the older generation of Negro leaders who sought through integration the dissolution of the Negro community, and the total assimilation of its members. Realistically, the elders recognized that the stubborn fact of pigmentation would make the goal more difficult to achieve than it had been for other minorities who had attained it—but integration was the preachment they had inherited from a line of white reformers stretching back to the Abolitionists, and they regarded the course of separate Negro action as tainted with the racism they were fighting against.

The rising leadership does not reject the philosophical concept of integration. Even more militantly than their elders the youngsters demand the right of total social mobility—to live and work and attend school in circumstances that are in accord with their means and ability, and without reference to their race. Yet, when they propose to break with the white and the white-oriented leadership and use the weight of Negro political and economic solidarity to pursue these goals, they are in fact accepting, if not segregation, at least separation.

The parallel most often cited is that of the earlier immigrants who occupied many of the same ghettos in which Negroes and Puerto Ricans are now huddled—the Jews, the Italians, the Irish, the Poles, and the Germans. These too were initially consigned to closed neighborhoods and menial employment. But within the ghettos they husbanded their resources, improved the opportunities for their children, and in time began the outward and upward movement that has led to their assimilation in the larger American community.

There are those—and not necessarily philosophical white supremacists—who doubt that the Negro temperament and prior conditioning will permit the development of similar patterns. They point to the fact that the primary elements that held the earlier communities together and gave them common purpose are missing in the case of the dark-skinned newcomers—a separate culture or religion or language. In the case of the Negro the attitudes long since imposed upon him in his years in the South are those of the white community, warped though they may have been by the practical impossibility of attaining the standards he was taught to respect.

It is this heritage of the dismal past that presently frustrates Negro leaders and feeds their resentment against the whites who fashioned it. In a sense the prior attain-

ments of non-Southern Negroes have been temporarily
overwhelmed by the great tides of immigration. Any
realistic appraisal of the urban ghettos has to begin with
the fact that a considerable majority of their residents are
so new to the cities they have not yet had time to over-
come the deficiencies of their earlier environment. A man
who is tasting new freedoms is more likely to be interested
in celebrating the present than in laying by stores for
the future. David B. Carlson has summarized the sociologists' estimate of these new contributors to America's urban problems in an article in *Architectural Forum:*

> White or colored, the new urbanites are usually
> young (a majority are in the 15–29 age group) and
> generally have several children. They are rural or
> small-town oriented, with social life centered on the
> family. They are often incredibly impoverished, by
> urban standards. Their values frequently lead to dif-
> ficult adjustment. Housing is likely to be less impor-
> tant to them than other things. Saving means little to
> them, for they have long been used to living from
> hand to mouth on an uncertain future. Thus, they
> are easy prey for the dollar-a-week installment sellers
> who load them up with the glittering toys of urban
> society—television, automatic dishwashers, hi-fi
> phonographs, and automobiles. In their original
> homes religion was generally wrapped in a revival-

meeting atmosphere, and the decorous, quiet nature
of urban religious experience is likely to seem tame
by comparison.

Out of his experience with Chicago's immigrants, Chairman Ely Aaron of the Mayor's Committee on New Residents has described them as "proud, clannish, sensitive
about their lack of education. They are suspicious and they
don't know this business of working with people."

The number of Negroes who have so far broken out of
this pattern is still proportionately small. The new middle
class is largely made up of those who have found a place
in professional, managerial, or white-collar occupations—
estimated at 12 per cent of the total in 1955, as against 42
per cent of whites in similar categories. This group provides the voice of Negro protest, but tends to couch it
in limited, personal terms; it is not yet large enough nor
of sufficient stability to provide effective leadership and
example for the restless and chaotic mass. Moreover, many
of its members, jealously guarding their new status, de-
liberately refuse to assume the burden. Edward Holmgren
of the Chicago Urban League says bluntly that "middle-
class Negroes have an absolute abhorrence for lower-class
Negroes. They feel the lower classes bring them into dis-
repute and opprobrium."

But this too is a familiar aspect of minority development and transition. There were also lace-curtain Irish

who for the same reasons had an absolute abhorrence of the rowdy and dissolute shanty Irish, and cultivated Jews who changed their names in an effort to put as much distance as they could between themselves and the noisy and grasping co-religionists they agreed deserved the epithet, "kike."

In any event it seems certain that the Negro middle class will grow, and that the ranks of the new arrivals will thin. The Negro migration has already passed its peak. Irene Taeuber of Princeton's Office of Population Research reports that "the great reservoirs of Negroes in Southern agriculture are so reduced that they can furnish only a fraction of the migrants of the future." The higher birth rate among nonwhites will doubtless continue to increase the proportion of urban colored population, but the majority of the rising generation will begin their adjustment to the city with the first drawn breath.

Oscar Handlin, the Harvard historian, who has summarized extensive social studies of Negroes and Puerto Ricans in the New York metropolitan area in *The Newcomers,* believes that the developing pattern of the future is likely to produce additional cohesive Negro communities —not the great slum concentrations of the present, but communities scattered through the spreading suburbs and offering a variety of accommodations in which Negro families can find housing in accord with their income level.

Handlin contends that this is not only a likely development but from every standpoint—including the Negro's
—a highly desirable one. Anyone who has had practical
experience in the field would agree that what Handlin
politely calls "the genuine problems of social disorder"
which now exist in the ghettos do not respond readily to
external efforts at reform. They demand, in his view, communal institutions created and controlled by Negroes
themselves.

If Handlin's thesis is correct, and also proves acceptable
to the new Negro leadership, it would greatly reduce the
greatest source of friction between whites and Negroes.
The contest with whites for jobs is only a minor factor
now, and this will continue to be the case if the economy
maintains its present rate of expansion. Casual contact
between whites and Negroes in places of public accommodation produces few incidents these days. The Negro runs
into his greatest frustration, and the most marked displays
of overt hostility, when he seeks a decent place to live in
virtually the only place he can find it—a white neighborhood.

"I think this kind of development is possible," one of the
young intellectuals has said of Handlin's prospectus. "But
it can't be thrust upon Negroes by the whites. We've got to
have the right to live where we please. Once we've got
that I suspect most of us will tend to group together volun-
tarily. After all, that's really the point of the argument—

that we're not different from other people, it's just that other people treat us differently."

There is confirmation, too, in the fears voiced by Ray Jones, the Harlem political leader, and other practical men of affairs in the district. In the wake of the New York slum clearance program a few rather elegant and expensive apartment houses have been built and others projected. While open to Negroes, the economic factor keeps the number of colored tenants to a minimum and the apartments tend to fill with well-to-do whites.

"If we don't watch out," Jones says, "the whites are likely to ease back in here and take Harlem away from us. After all, it's the most attractive piece of real estate in the whole area. We've got hills and views of both rivers, the transportation is good, and it's the only close-in section that doesn't have any industry. If that happened we'd have some token integration for the Negro fat cats, but all those who couldn't afford high rents would be shunted off into some new slum."

It is doubtful that the circle will ever close in such ironic fashion and that Harlem will again become the high-fashion retreat for whites it was before the first Adam Clayton Powell moved the Abyssinian Baptist Church uptown and began the process that was to displace Commodore Vanderbilt and Colonel Kip Rhinelander, who exercised their trotting horses on Lenox Avenue, and the elegant neighbors who took their ease in handsome brownstones designed by Stanford White.

In the period of transition ahead—and no one can accurately estimate its duration—the Negro ghetto is certain to be a fixture of the American city. So long as it survives it will pose special problems and, more importantly, it will stand as a constant challenge to a democratic system under which it is palpably intolerable.

Already the time is past when the dominant white community could salve its conscience with ministrations of mercy and charity. Many depressed Negroes still stand in the need of such services, and of prayer too for that matter, but white largesse is no longer psychologically acceptable. Increasingly the Negro is insisting on standing on his own feet, and this seems a healthy and hopeful sign—painful though it certainly is to many whites who quite correctly diagnose it as a pressing threat to the status quo.

We are all, white and black alike, in for a nervous time. In a brief moment in our history the Negro's aspirations have leaped far ahead of the means presently available for their achievement. The deficiencies exist on both sides of the color line. The barriers of prejudice provide real inhibitions on the Negro's progress, but they also provide a too-handy excuse for his personal failures. The national Negro leadership, fighting with marked effectiveness to establish the minority's rights, has as yet shown little disposition to assume matching responsibility for the im-

154 · THE OTHER SIDE OF JORDAN

provement of internal affairs within the Negro communities. The effort to alleviate the human erosion of poverty, ignorance and crime still comes primarily from whites. It has been largely ineffective, and will continue to be, for the reasons pointed out by Oscar Handlin in support of his thesis that the worst of these internal problems will yield only to communal institutions maintained by Negroes on their own terms.

There is presently something approximating a leadership vacuum at the community level. We may assume that it will be filled in time from the ranks of the younger Negroes now taking their place in the expanding middle class. But this will be an uneven, and sometimes painful process; the white community must recognize, as it has not yet, that the capacity for leadership is developed only through practice. There are mistakes still to be made, probably monumental ones—and even the strongest of the new Negro leaders must be expected to yield expediently to the powerful emotional pressures of their community's special grievances, pent up for generations and now released in full force.

The drive to resolve the race problem must proceed simultaneously on two levels. We must employ all the urban renewal tools now at hand, and some yet to be devised, to improve the environment within the ghettos. At the same time we must accelerate the effort to reduce the white prejudice that denies the Negro the social mobility accorded all other Americans. The heaviest burden of the first task falls upon the Negro, that of the second upon the white. Yet there is an inherent interaction between the two; improvement in the condition of Negroes, as individuals and in the mass, reduces the white resistance to association on terms of full equality; acceptance of some Negroes on such terms fires the ambition of the rest by demonstrating that the course of self-improvement no longer has an arbitrary limit.

A perfect solution will doubtless have to wait upon a change in the hearts and minds of men, as President Eisenhower insisted in attempting to justify the eight years of inaction the historians may count as the greatest domestic failure of his administration. But steady progress toward that solution cannot await the millennium. We are enjoined to it by considerations of morality, as we always have been. But this is also a practical matter of great urgency. The agrarian past is finished; the heart of our nation is in the great cities now, and they are afflicted with a grave disease.

It is here that we must seek the terms of racial peace and justice in the fateful second half of the century.